Y0-BZG-911

05°

DATE DUE			

DISCARD

J 363.9
HAE

Birth Control

Other Books of Related Interest:

At Issue Series

Age of Consent

Are Abortion Rights Threatened?

Do Abstinence Programs Work?

Global Viewpoints Series

Human Rights

Opposing Viewpoints Series

Human Rights

Parenting

Women's Health

GLOBALVIEWPOINTS

Birth Control

Margaret Haerens, Book Editor

GREENHAVEN PRESS
A part of Gale, Cengage Learning

GALE
CENGAGE Learning·

Farmington Hills, Mich • San Francisco • New York • Waterville, Maine
Meriden, Conn • Mason, Ohio • Chicago

Elizabeth Des Chenes, *Director, Content Strategy*
Cynthia Sanner, *Publisher*
Douglas Dentino, *Manager, New Product*

© 2014 Greenhaven Press, a part of Gale, Cengage Learning

WCN: 01-100-101

Articles in Greenhaven Press anthologies are often edited for length to meet page requirements. In addition, original titles of these works are changed to clearly present the main thesis and to explicitly indicate the author's opinion. Every effort is made to ensure that Greenhaven Press accurately reflects the original intent of the authors. Every effort has been made to trace the owners of copyrighted material.

Cover image © Ocean/Corbis.

LIBRARY OF CONGRESS CATALOGING-IN-PUBLICATION DATA

Birth control / Margaret Haerens, book editor.
    pages cm. -- (Global viewpoints)
    Includes bibliographical references and index.
    ISBN 978-0-7377-6260-0 (hardcover) -- ISBN 978-0-7377-6436-9 (pbk.)
    1. Birth control. 2. Birth control--United States. I. Haerens, Margaret.
    HQ766.B4794 2014
    363.9'60973--dc23
                                                                    2013029610

Printed in Mexico
2 3 4 5 6 7 18 17 16 15 14

Contents

Turkey's fertility rate has declined because of more favorable economic conditions, a rising level of female education, and greater use of birth control. However, the fertility rates among the Kurdish population are much higher and may lead to a Kurdish majority in Turkey in about thirty years.

Chapter 2: Politics and Birth Control

The morality of birth control became a key issue in the US presidential race after a controversy erupted over a proposal on contraceptive health coverage. Limiting access to birth control for women was a contentious issue during the election.

Senegal's rapid population growth, high poverty rates, and levels of maternal mortality should have made family planning programs a priority. In recent years, however, much of the money to fund such programs was used to fight HIV/AIDS instead.

Chapter 3: Social and Religious Factors Affecting Access to Birth Control

Chapter 4: The Economics of Birth Control Access

The Chilean government is working to make emergency contraception accessible and affordable to women who need it, despite a court ruling that prohibits its free distribution. Health care authorities believe that such efforts will reduce the skyrocketing number of illegal abortions and teenage pregnancies in Chile.

Foreword

> "The problems of all of humanity can
> only be solved by all of humanity."
> —Swiss author Friedrich Dürrenmatt

Global interdependence has become an undeniable reality.
Mass media and technology have increased worldwide
access to information and created a society of global citizens.
Understanding and navigating this global community is a
challenge, requiring a high degree of information literacy and
a new level of learning sophistication.

Building on the success of its flagship series, Opposing
Viewpoints, Greenhaven Press has created the Global Viewpoints series to examine a broad range of current, often controversial topics of worldwide importance from a variety of
international perspectives. Providing students and other readers with the information they need to explore global connec-
tions and think critically about worldwide implications, each
Global Viewpoints volume offers a panoramic view of a topic
of widespread significance.

Drugs, famine, immigration—a broad, international treatment is essential to do justice to social, environmental, health,
and political issues such as these. Junior high, high school,
and early college students, as well as general readers, can all
use Global Viewpoints anthologies to discern the complexities
relating to each issue. Readers will be able to examine unique
national perspectives while, at the same time, appreciating the
interconnectedness that global priorities bring to all nations
and cultures.

Material in each volume is selected from a diverse range of
sources, including journals, magazines, newspapers, nonfiction
books, speeches, government documents, pamphlets, organiza-

11

tion newsletters, and position papers. Global Viewpoints is truly global, with material drawn primarily from international sources available in English and secondarily from US sources with extensive international coverage.

Features of each volume in the Global Viewpoints series include:

- An **annotated table of contents** that provides a brief summary of each essay in the volume, including the name of the country or area covered in the essay.

- An **introduction** specific to the volume topic.

- A **world map** to help readers locate the countries or areas covered in the essays.

- For each viewpoint, an **introduction** that contains notes about the author and source of the viewpoint explains why material from the specific country is being presented, summarizes the main points of the viewpoint, and offers three **guided reading questions** to aid in understanding and comprehension.

- **For further discussion** questions that promote critical thinking by asking the reader to compare and contrast aspects of the viewpoints or draw conclusions about perspectives and arguments.

- A worldwide list of **organizations to contact** for readers seeking additional information.

- A **periodical bibliography** for each chapter and a **bibliography of books** on the volume topic to aid in further research.

- A comprehensive **subject index** to offer access to people, places, events, and subjects cited in the text, with the countries covered in the viewpoints highlighted.

Global Viewpoints is designed for a broad spectrum of readers who want to learn more about current events, history, political science, government, international relations, economics, environmental science, world cultures, and sociology—students doing research for class assignments or debates, teachers and faculty seeking to supplement course materials, and others wanting to understand current issues better. By presenting how people in various countries perceive the root causes, current consequences, and proposed solutions to worldwide challenges, Global Viewpoints volumes offer readers opportunities to enhance their global awareness and their knowledge of cultures worldwide.

Introduction

"Family planning is one of the most critical services needed to manage population growth, to complete the demographic transition and to achieve a demographic dividend."

—*"Planning Population Dynamics for Growth and Development," International Planned Parenthood Federation, July 2012*

Since ancient times, birth control has been used by women and men as a tool to exercise their reproductive freedom and avoid unwanted pregnancy. On an individual level, it allows women a chance to limit the number of times they get pregnant over their lifetimes, impacting both rates of maternal mortality and infant mortality. Childbirth is fraught with physical danger, often resulting in the death of mother or child—or even both. Women bearing large numbers of children often experience health problems from frequent pregnancies and the physical toll of breast-feeding and child rearing. Children born into large families may also deal with health problems and compete for resources, making them vulnerable to childhood diseases or other health issues. Parents have to provide for large families; this can be a serious financial strain on couples with limited funds and economic opportunities.

On a community, regional, or national level, contraception is a way to control population growth and population dynamics, which refers to the characteristics of a specific population. Population dynamics have a profound impact on the health of an economy and human development. A balanced community, one not burdened with an overwhelming majority of one age group or gender, has a better chance of survival and prosperity over the long term. In the twentieth century, many governments made population dynamics and contraceptive policy key priorities as concerns about overpopulation and depleting resources increased. Government planning became essential to controlling population growth—and access to birth control was key to such broad family planning efforts. Limiting access to birth control and encouraging procreation should lead to population growth; conversely, broadening access to birth control and discouraging procreation should reduce population growth.

In ancient times, authorities prioritized security and looked to maintain populations large and healthy enough to defend the community from attack. In approximately 300 BCE, the political philosopher and royal advisor Chanakya advocated for policies to increase the population of the Maurya Empire in southern India by allowing widows to remarry (a practice forbidden at that time) and discouraging asceticism, a spiritual lifestyle that dictates abstinence and refraining from any sexual activity. Ancient Greek philosophers, including Plato and Aristotle, debated the issue of population growth and the challenge of maintaining the optimal population dynamics for political, economic, and military strength. In his writings, Aristotle recognized that unchecked population growth could lead to poverty—and poverty could lead to violence, crime, and even rebellion. He advocated for abortion and infanticide as ways to control population growth in Greek city-states.

In ancient Rome, a series of population measures were enacted to spur population growth, which was needed to maintain the large Roman army and its frequent excursions. Men and women received employment and tax advantages to marry early and have large families. In a number of societies, female or disabled infants were abandoned and left to die or sold into slavery to curb overpopulation or maintain a certain population dynamic. Deadly disease, famine, and natural disasters were also viewed as God's, or nature's, way of dealing with overpopulation.

In 1798 Thomas Malthus, a British clergyman and economist, published an influential treatise on population control, *An Essay on the Principle of Population*, in which he argued that birth control was a vital preventative check on high birthrates. Malthus contends that overpopulation exacerbates poverty and makes it more difficult to attain economic stability. To better their economic opportunities, Malthus advocated that the lower classes should practice moral restraint and abstinence to decrease the birthrate.

In modern times, many nations have adopted stringent birth control policies to control population growth. China's one-child policy is one of the most controversial. Under the Communist regime of Mao Zedong, government officials encouraged population growth in order to attain greater economic, political, and military power. By 1970, however, government officials recognized the strain of the country's rapid population increase and were encouraging couples to marry later and have only two children. When the government realized that the decline in fertility rates was not enough, it implemented a one-child policy in 1979: Couples in urban areas were allowed only one child; in rural areas, where children are often needed to work on farms, families were allowed more than one child if the first one was a girl or physically or mentally impaired. Families violating the one-child policy were subject to large fines, meaning that rich families were able to skirt the law. There were other penalties, including a loss of employment opportunities, economic disincentives, and social sanctions. However, in recent years there have been many adjustments to the policy, and enforcement has been lax in many areas.

China's one-child policy had an effect on the country's population dynamics. The fertility rate in China dropped from 2.63 births per woman in 1980 to 1.61 per woman in 2009. Chinese authorities claim that the drop allowed the country's rapid economic development and rise to economic power. They argue that controlling population growth resulted in less poverty, disease, environmental damage, and strain on natural resources.

The cultural preference for male children in China has also had a profound effect on the country's population dynamics. Until the late 1990s, infanticide and abandonment of female babies occurred, according to observers. Access to ultrasounds, which identify sex characteristics of the fetus, has led to a trend of sex-selective abortions. As a result, there is a wide gender disparity in China, with many more men than women. According to a report published by the National Health and Family Planning Commission, there will be thirty million more men of marriageable age than women by 2020. It also warned that such a gender disparity could cause social instability and other problems.

Critics charge that the one-child policy has led to terrible abuses. One of the most heinous is allegations of forced abortions. Another is forced sterilizations of women. Both practices were outlawed in 2002, but it is reported that forced abortions and sterilizations continue in some areas. Many critics assert that the one-child policy leads to an economic strain on the child, who is responsible for financially supporting his or her parents and grandparents.

In recent years, the Chinese government has announced that it will review the one-child policy. The release of China's 2010 census, which shows a much more pronounced decline in the birthrate than estimated, only intensified calls for an end to the controversial policy. The drop ignited concerns that China's aging labor market will halt economic development and inhibit entrepreneurship. It is predicted that the Chinese government will eliminate the one-child policy in the next few years.

The authors of the viewpoints included in *Global Viewpoints: Birth Control* explore the connection between birth control and population growth, as well as the government's role in family planning. Other subjects include the impact of religious, social, and cultural factors on the availability and popularity of contraception; the ways in which politics determine family planning policies; and the economic considerations that influence birth control and family planning decisions.

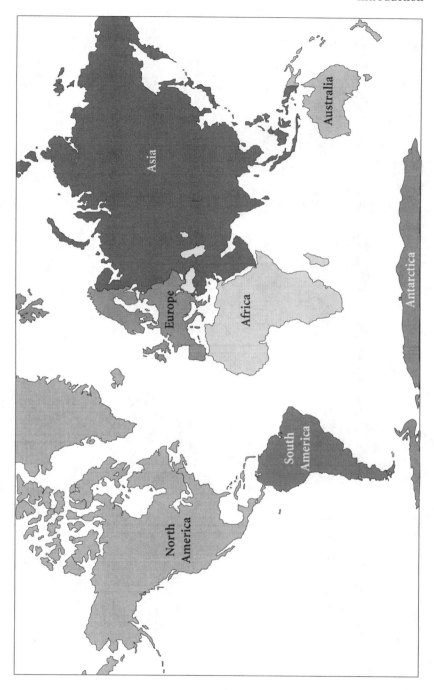

CHAPTER 1

Birth Control and Population Growth

The Myth of 9 Billion

Malcolm Potts and Martha Campbell

Malcolm Potts is a professor at the School of Public Health at the University of California, Berkeley. Martha Campbell is a resident at Venture Strategies for Health and Development and a lecturer at the University of California, Berkeley. In the following viewpoint, they contend that the shift away from effective family planning policies in developing countries in the 1990s has led to revisions of world population growth estimates. As access to contraception has become more limited in developing countries, population growth has increased. This trend will have a profound effect on life in the next century, straining food and fresh water supplies and increasing rates of poverty, starvation, and illness. International authorities still have the opportunity to address the potential demographic time bomb by emphasizing family planning and improving access to contraception in regions such as sub-Saharan Africa.

As you read, consider the following questions:

1. According to the United Nations Population Division, what will be the global population by the end of this century?
2. According to Babatunde Osotimehin, how many women in developing countries need access to modern contraception?

3. What do the authors believe that the world population could be by 2050 if the right measures are taken now?

This week the United Nations Population Division made a radical shift in its population projections. Previously, the organization had estimated that the number of people living on the planet would reach around 9 billion by 2050—and then level off. Now everything has changed: Rather than leveling off, the population size will continue to grow, reaching 10 billion or more at century's end.

Why is this happening? Put simply, fertility rates. Across much of the world, women are having fewer children, but in African countries, the decline is far slower than expected. Part of this shift was supposed to come from preferences about family size and better access to family planning to make that possible. Sadly, however, that access hasn't come. Another factor, many expected, would come from the deleterious impact of high HIV/AIDS rates. But even Uganda—with one of the highest numbers of AIDS cases in sub-Saharan Africa—is projected to almost triple its population by 2050. In fact, outside a handful of countries, HIV/AIDS has only a tiny impact on overall population. Consider this: In the first five months of this year, the world population grew by enough to equal all the AIDS deaths since the epidemic began 30 years ago.

Rapid population growth is bad news for the continent, as it will likely outstrip gains in economic development. It's also a wake-up call: If the world doesn't begin investing far more seriously in family planning, much of our progress fighting poverty in sub-Saharan Africa over the last half century could be lost.

Demographic projections are just that—predictions. They only tell us what can happen if we make a variety of policy decisions and investments. As is the case with these projections, they include a lower and higher estimate—and where we end up in that range depends upon what we do in the meantime. Hence, it would be a mistake to focus only on the medium U.N. projection of 9.3 billion people by 2050 as most commentators do. The high projection would take us to 10.6 billion in 2050. The low projection would mean 8.1 billion. (Just for a sense of scale: The difference between these high and low variants is equivalent to the entire global population in 1950.)

That 2050 figure is vital in determining how large the population will grow by 2100—either as high as 15.8 billion or as low as 6.2 billion. With so many people reproducing, very small differences in family size have a dramatic impact over time. The difference between a world of 6.2 billion and 15.8 billion will depend on a change in the average number of children that women have—a change that is so small that demographers are reduced to using the odd image of "half a child" to describe it. Over the coming 40 years, however, if the average woman bears half a child more, on average, it will have an almost unimaginably profound effect on virtually everything else that happens in the 21st century.

Oddly, for a world in which information travels so quickly, access to contraceptives—and information about family planning—is extremely hard to come by in large parts of Africa.

Let's imagine how different our world could look, depending upon its population. Already, we face a host of challenges: feeding growing numbers of middle-class meat-eating citizens, lifting the bottom third of the world's people out of poverty, and ensuring that our ever-growing economies are environmentally sustainable. All these necessities will become more urgent and more difficult if the population grows quickly, particularly in poor countries where adequate food supplies and sufficient sources of water often can't be taken for granted.

Some of the countries in sub-Saharan Africa, especially those making up the Sahel bordering the Sahara desert, face particularly somber demographic problems. In Niger, the rate of population growth exceeds economic growth. Twenty percent of women there have 10 or more children, and only one in 1,000 women completes secondary school. Already, one-third of children in Niger are malnourished, and global warming will further undermine agricultural output in the desertifying Sahel. Even if the current birthrate is halved by 2050, the population will still explode—from 14 million today to 53 million by 2050. If the birthrate continues at current levels, the population could reach a totally unsustainable 80 million. Unless there is an immediate commitment to family planning, the scale of human suffering over the next three decades in the Sahel could equal or exceed that caused by HIV/AIDS in the past 30 years.

Why are some countries having such a difficult time reducing their average family size? Oddly, for a world in which information travels so quickly, access to contraceptives—and information about family planning—is extremely hard to come by in large parts of Africa. A poor woman who cannot obtain contraception will have many children, and often not by choice. Often, the contraceptives themselves simply aren't in supply; other times, there are barriers—such as government or medical regulations and misinformation—that prevent access.

Ironically, the future problem stems from today's success: Women are not having more children than in the past, but fewer of them are dying. Globally, the number of infant deaths per 1,000 births fell from 126 in 1960 to 57 in 2001.

Persistently high fertility yields some striking statistics, according to Babatunde Osotimehin, the executive director of the U.N. Population Fund (UNFPA). Last month he called for urgent action to meet the needs of "some 215 million women in developing countries, who want to plan and space their

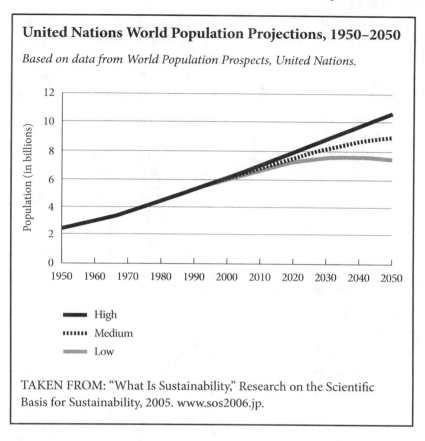

United Nations World Population Projections, 1950–2050

Based on data from World Population Prospects, United Nations.

Legend:
- High
- Medium
- Low

TAKEN FROM: "What Is Sustainability," Research on the Scientific Basis for Sustainability, 2005. www.sos2006.jp.

births, [but] do not have access to modern contraception." He added that "neglect of sexual and reproductive health results in an estimated 80 million unintended pregnancies; 22 million unsafe abortions; and 358,000 deaths from maternal causes—including 47,000 deaths from unsafe abortion."

That so many women lack access to family planning may come as a surprise to many who have watched women's rights improve throughout the world in recent decades. But after much attention to population control in the 1970s, interest began to wane in the 1990s. Below-replacement fertility levels in countries such as Russia and Japan suggested the much-heralded population explosion was over. Then, in 1994, an influential International Conference on Population and Development (ICPD) in Cairo emphasized the need to focus on the many needs of girls and women, including health care, education, economic opportunity, the ability to own property, and freedom from domestic violence, as well as access to family planning. It was a worthy goal to work toward these broader needs, but as a result of advocacy, the word "population" became tainted with the idea that improving access to birth control was tantamount to coercion. The term "family planning" was replaced by the broader phrase "reproductive health." In the United States, in particular, passions over abortion eroded support for contraceptives assistance overseas.

That lack of attention may well prove to be one of the worst foreign policy mistakes of recent decades. Budgets for family planning have collapsed—despite the fact that they were yielding real results. When a modest investment was made in family planning in Kenya in the 1980s, for example, the average family size fell from eight to five. When the focus was taken off family planning, this decline stalled and even started rising again. In 1990, demographers had predicted the population of Kenya in 2050 would be 53 million. But now, the population in 2050 is predicted to be 65 million. This extra 12 million people is equivalent to twice the total population of the whole country in 1950.

If we want to live in an ecologically sustainable world, we'll have to meet the needs of the present without compromising the natural resources and services our children and grandchildren will need.

In Kenya, the richest economic quintiles have three children, while the poorest have eight. Rich women use contraception more frequently than poor women, but the poor have almost three times the unmet need for family planning— women who report that they do not want another child in the next two years but are not using contraception. It is not that the poor want more children to help in the fields or look after elders as they age; they simply don't have access to family planning options and information they need and deserve.

Rapid population growth inhibits many of the factors of development from proceeding apace—including education and health. In all our research, we have not found any country, with the exception of a few oil-rich states, that has developed or extricated itself from poverty while maintaining high average family size. Countries with high birthrates tend to find it difficult or impossible to expand their education systems or their health systems adequately to keep up with the need.

This matters beyond any one country or region. If we want to live in an ecologically sustainable world, we'll have to meet the needs of the present without compromising the natural resources and services our children and grandchildren will need. Given time, and a great deal of scientific ingenuity, we might still be able to reduce our consumption and pull a world of 8 billion people back to a biologically sustainable economy by the end of the century. But a world of 10 billion more in 2050 could do irreversible damage to the planet. It's just too many people.

We've now been warned. If measures are taken now, we could still keep the 2050 world population at around 8 billion. We have to ensure that the population can be slowed by purely voluntary means and within a human rights framework. We need to galvanize the political will to make it happen and invest now so that family planning options are universally available. Fail to do so and we may give birth to a new, difficult era of poverty instead.

Global Population Growth Is Relatively Unaffected by the Availability of Birth Control

Dominic Lawson

Dominic Lawson is a columnist for the Times *(London). In the following viewpoint, he suggests that the birth of the seven billionth person on the planet should be a cause for celebration, not for concern. Lawson argues that activists exaggerate the problem of population growth and finds that society has been creative and productive enough to find solutions to the challenges of a rising global population. He also contends that large-scale family planning programs and the increased availability of birth control in developing countries will have little to no effect on the rates of population growth because family planning has more to do with individual choice than international population edicts.*

As you read, consider the following questions:

1. When was Adnan Nevic born, according to Lawson?
2. When did the United Nations determine that the world's seven billionth person would be born?
3. What did the author Fred Pearce discover about the rural African community of Machakos while researching his book?

Does the name Adnan Nevic mean anything to you? Twelve years ago his birth was quite an event.

A Media Circus

Kofi Annan, then the United Nations [UN] secretary-general, flew in to Sarajevo University's clinical centre to be photographed holding the baby only moments after his birth at 12:04 a.m. local time, October 12, 1999.

The motive for this peculiar media circus was that the UN had determined the planet's 6 billionth living human was to be born that day—and Sarajevo won the lucky dip.

UN officials insisted that the fact that the city had only recently recovered from a dreadful civil war was "purely coincidental" to its choice of venue. Anyway, Fatima Nevic was the first mother in Sarajevo's main maternity hospital to give birth on the designated day and, as a result, the boy resignedly remarked recently, "everyone strokes my head and then they disappear".

The fact that we humans are about to breach the 7 billion barrier is the clearest refutation of that bleak underestimation of the creative power of our species.

The 7 Billion Mark

Now—how time flies—the UN's ever-active population division is girding itself to mark the birth of the planet's 7 billionth living soul. This time it has determined a due date of October 31 [2011], although the venue of this supposititious event has not yet been revealed by the UN's imaginative public relations folk—perhaps they will let us know this week, so the world's media have time to book suitable hotels for correspondents. The chances are, however, that there may not be much five-star accommodation in the chosen vicinity. The *Financial Times* has declared the appropriate venue would be "a ramshackle hut in the suburbs of Nairobi", which, it observes, "is crowded, polluted and crime-ridden".

This is characteristic of the moroseness—and even despair—with which this event is being marked. It is Malthusians who now seem to be multiplying like rabbits, with few able to see a 7 billionth human as a cause for celebration—and not just for the parents in question. When Thomas Malthus, in his *An Essay on the Principle of Population*, declared the world already had too many mouths to feed and there was no possibility of sufficient food being produced to meet the demands created by further growth in the population, the number of humans was no more than 1 billion. Like his later imitators—in 1968 Paul Ehrlich's undeservedly influential book *The Population Bomb* stated as fact that by the end of that century even the United States would be in the grip of mass famine—Malthus assumed the limits of agricultural productivity had been reached and the more we became, the less we would have to eat.

Reassessing Population Growth

The fact that we humans are about to breach the 7 billion barrier is the clearest refutation of that bleak underestimation of the creative power of our species. As that true visionary Peter Bauer pointed out when Ehrlich was in high fashion, the so-called population explosion "should be seen as a blessing rather than a disaster, because it stems from a fall in mortality, a prima facie improvement in people's welfare". Bauer would not have been at all surprised that India, now the world's second most populous nation, has for some years been a net exporter of grain—even though, according to Ehrlich, they should all have been wiped out by famine, being unable to feed themselves, let alone anyone else.

David Attenborough, a fellow patron with Ehrlich of Population Matters (a body devoted to reducing the number of humans), recently declared that "there is no human problem

© Paul Fell/www.cartoonstock.com.

that is not directly made worse by population growth". He excludes from this misanthropic analysis the thought that, along with all our wickedness, humans are also the creators of everything that is good, innovative and brilliant in the world; it is a result of that ingenuity and creativity that both medicine and agriculture have advanced dramatically—and thus our overall numbers.

Machakos's Population Thrives

In fact, it is only in sub-Saharan Africa that populations are still growing at significantly above replacement rate; and Englishmen since the days of empire have been prone to the view that the inhabitants of that continent are too many for their own good. In *More People, Less Erosion* the geographer Michael Mortimore and the development economist Mary Tiffen examined the Kenyan rural district of Machakos. They chose this area because it had been stigmatised by their colonial soil scientist predecessors as "an appalling example" of incipient environmental disaster: This had been blamed on "multiplication of the natives", whose land was degenerating into "a parched desert of rocks, stone and sand".

Yet, as Mortimore and Tiffen noted, it was because of population growth that the inhabitants of Machakos had the human resources, without any assistance from the British, to dig terraces to reduce soil erosion and create sand dams to capture rainwater.

Invariably, it is private choice that determines [family size], not birth control instructions from higher powers and especially not those from other nations.

When Fred Pearce visited Machakos while researching his recent book *Peoplequake*, he discovered the subsistence farmers written off 80 years earlier by the Malthusian colonialists were "producing so much food that they were selling vegetables and milk in Nairobi, mangoes and oranges to the Middle East, avocados to France and green beans to Britain".

Nothing daunted by the facts, the population doomsters assert that all the wars in Africa are about a scramble for food on the part of tribes unconstrained by Western-style birth control: It is routinely claimed that the Rwandan civil war was a fight over diminishing resources among a rapidly growing population of rival Hutus and Tutsis. As Pearce points out in his indispensable book, food production in Rwanda had grown by almost 5% a year in the decades before the massacres, significantly more than the rate of population growth. It is wars that have created such famines as have occurred in Africa, much though it suits some in the population reduction lobby to confuse cause with effect.

The Exaggerated Role of Family Planning and Contraception

This is not an argument for a Vatican-style edict against artificial birth control. However, the sort of mass condom drop favoured by the likes of Ehrlich and Attenborough will have no great effect on family sizes. Invariably, it is private choice that determines such matters, not birth control instructions from higher powers and especially not those from other nations.

With the possible (and brutal) exception of China, the UN Population Division's own figures demonstrate that in countries where fertility rates have fallen markedly there has been no great difference in the rate of decline whether governments have promoted birth control or not. There are only two statistically watertight correlations: Fertility rates fall almost exactly as female literacy rises; and the more urbanised a country becomes, the smaller is the average family.

These are the twin phenomena behind the real story obscured by the palaver over the 7 billionth human: a sustained, unpredicted and dramatic worldwide decline in global fertility rates. While we are now familiar with the idea that western Europe, Russia and Japan are all having to deal with the social consequences of an ageing and diminishing population, even countries as diverse as Brazil, Thailand and Tunisia are now in a demographic downward spiral.

China, meanwhile, is having to face up to the true long-term consequences of its draconian population reduction policies (which so impressed the UN Population Division in the 1980s that it gave medals to the instigators of forced abortions): a grotesquely disproportionate male majority and the prospect of being the first country to become old before it is rich. State-backed euthanasia is just one possible consequence.

This week, however, we should turn away from such sad thoughts and raise our glasses to the arrival of the 7 billionth human living among us. Haven't we done well?

China's Strict Birth Control Policy Is Leading to an Aging Population

Tania Branigan

Tania Branigan is a foreign correspondent for the Guardian. *In the following viewpoint, she investigates the challenges of China's demographic outlook, which shows a growing elderly population and a shrinking number of young adults to help take care of them. Branigan finds that as life expectancy has improved, more Chinese citizens are living to an older age. Meanwhile, strict birth control policies have led to a declining birthrate. This demographic problem will have wide-ranging economic, social, and political consequences. Branigan explains that one solution is to eliminate the one-child policy and allow couples to have two children, a move that would go a long way to alleviating the demographic problem.*

As you read, consider the following questions:

1. According to the estimates, what will be the population of people over the age of sixty in China by 2050?
2. How many only children are there in China, according to Branigan?

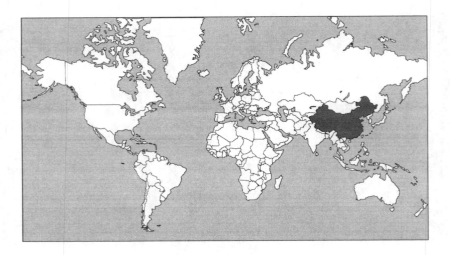

3. According to the World Bank, China has enough care
homes for what percentage of its aging population?

While hundreds of millions of Chinese families toasted
the new year together, 84-year-old He Daxing huddled
on the doorstep of his daughter's home in Chongqing.

On the most important date in the calendar, not one of
his six grown children—born before the country's one-child
policy was imposed—would take him in.

Filial piety is so embedded here that officials offered to
help him sue his offspring when he fell ill after four nights
outside: Chinese law requires adults to support their parents.
Yet his case shows that traditional ideals are under growing
pressure in a fast-changing, increasingly individualistic society.

China may soon have more He Daxings. It faces a soaring
number of old people and a shrinking number of young
adults, who are also less able—and sometimes less willing—to
support their elders.

A Demographic "Timebomb"

Life expectancy has soared in China, while fertility has plummeted due to strict birth control policies. In 2009 there were
167 million over-60s, about an eighth of the population. By

2050 there will be 480 million, while the number of young people will have fallen. "It's a timebomb," warned Wang Feng of the Brookings-Tsinghua Center for Public Policy in Beijing.

China's economic miracle has been fuelled by its "demographic dividend": an unusually high proportion of working-age citizens. That population bulge is becoming a problem as it ages. In 2000 there were six workers for every over-60. By 2030, there will be barely two.

Other countries are also ageing and have far lower birth-rates. But China is the first to face the issue before it has developed—and the shift is two to three times as fast.

"China is unique: She is getting older before she has got rich," said Wang Dewen, of the World Bank's China social protection team.

Life expectancy has soared in China, while fertility has plummeted due to strict birth control policies.

Urban Migration

Tens of millions of workers have migrated to the cities, creating an even worse imbalance in rural areas which already suffer low incomes, poor public services and minimal social security.

Most old people there rely on their own labour and their children. China not only needs to support more older people for longer, but to extend support to new parts of society. World Bank researchers point to promising advances, such as the national rural pension scheme and the expansion of health insurance.

China can help deal with increased costs by raising its retirement age; at present, only about a fifth of urban women are still working at 55. Improving education should also raise productivity. Some experts believe such measures will be enough to wipe out the "demographic debt". Others wonder if China will begin to welcome immigrants.

Wang Feng thinks China has been far too timid, storing up trouble for the future. "Leaders have ridden the economic boom and largely collected and spent money and built infrastructure—the hardware: railroads, bridges," he said.

"[In the future] they will not have the money to spend, but what is more challenging is the part policy makers have stayed away from: building software—the pensions and health care system. That will be critical to social stability and regime legitimacy, but it is much harder to do."

In many ways, China is a good place to age.

Tackling Fertility Rates

The current five-year plan is the first to address ageing. But Wang said leaders had yet to accept it also meant tackling fertility. Under the "one-child policy"—which has several exemptions—the fertility rate has dropped to between 1.5 and 1.8, say experts. That is well below the 2.1 figure required to keep the population stable.

Many experts have urged the government to move to a uniform two-child policy. Instead, it has extended what was meant to be a one-generation measure.

China's 150 million children face a heavier burden of duties, but economic changes such as migration make them harder to fulfill.

Cultural Shifts

In many ways, China is a good place to age. Older people tend to be active, involved and respected community members. Family bonds remain strong.

"Having undutiful children or being an undutiful child is something really shameful in Chinese culture," said Dr Feng-shu Liu of Oslo University, who has researched intergenerational relationships.

China's Family Planning

With a population estimated in 2011 at more than 1.3 billion, China is the most populous nation in the world. There are dozens of minority groups, but 91.5% of the population is Han Chinese. The population is mainly focused in the east, with the most densely populated areas along the coast. An estimated 47% of the population was living in cities in 2010. Life expectancy is 74.7 years.

Since the 1970s, the government has emphasized family planning, imposing a "one-child rule" on most families. As a result, population growth has been significantly reduced, but the one-child rule has created a dramatic shift in the balance between the number of male and female births. As more couples prefer to have male offspring, there has been an increase in the number of sex-selective abortions and adoptions of female infants. A study released in April 2009 reported that there were 32 million more boys than girls among the Chinese population age 20 and under.

"China," Global Issues in Context
Online Collection, 2012.

Society has moved away from the "top-down, authoritarian" family model, but still expects children to meet their parents' physical and emotional needs and often to support them financially.

Several of the young people she interviewed saw filial piety as a basic requirement in a spouse.

Officials have been keen to promote such ideals—some have even pushed for laws ordering children to visit regularly—and not just for economic reasons, Liu argued. They see it as helping to preserve stability and social co-operation.

In a more individualistic society, relationships face new challenges. Children and their spouses can find their parents' demands excessive or intrusive.

He Daxing's daughters complained he had favoured his sons. And even when personal relations are good, practicalities may intervene. Children may work far from their parents, like one of He's sons, or simply lack time to help.

Demands of Modern Life

"I have one daughter and there's no way she will be able to take care of me. I will be in a care home when I get older," predicted Liu Zhongli.

Her pragmatism is unusual, but then Liu is director of Evergreen, a state-owned old people's home in north Beijing. She says that children still love their parents—her facility is inundated with visitors each weekend—but that the pressures of modern life are often overwhelming. "Even if your parents live with you, every day you leave early and come back from work late—so you still leave them at home alone. That's not support and that's not filial," she said.

Increased life expectancy can also mean children need care themselves, like the 88-year-old son of the home's oldest resident, who has just turned 109.

For many, there is still a stigma in moving into a care home. But 86-year-old Zhang Jiazhen tried living with her daughters in the US and said she is happier in Evergreen. "I'm an independent person . . . I really don't like China's old-fashioned view that you raise sons and daughters to support you when you're old," she said. "I can mix with a bigger family here."

The facilities are modern and comfortable and the atmosphere companionable. Retirees sing together or battle it out at billiard and mahjong tables.

Meeting Demographic Challenges

But even if you can afford Evergreen's fees of up to 5,100 yuan (£510) each month, it has just 600 beds, and a waiting list of 1,300. According to the World Bank, China has only enough care home places for 1.6% of over-60s, while in developed countries the capacity is about 8%.

Many of those homes are grim and there is a desperate shortage of good staff: Most are unskilled or have little training.

Evergreen is a testing ground for potential solutions. A team from Beijing Aeronautics and Astronautics University are trialing a bed that turns into a wheelchair, giving residents more independence, and a robot "dog" to keep them company. "The robot can have simple chats with them, play music and opera, or even dance for them through sound controls. It says 'It feels so good!' when they pet it," said researcher Zhang Guanxin.

But while such innovations may smooth the later years of wealthier urban citizens, the poor will need help from China's leaders to meet basic needs. Even then, argues Wang Feng, families will face extra strain.

"People who could have had a second child [were it not for the one-child policy] have missed the opportunity and when they grow older it is not clear how the government can come to the rescue. In fact, I think it's clear that the government cannot substitute for families," he said.

A Kurdish Majority in Turkey Within One Generation?

Palash R. Ghosh

Palash R. Ghosh is a writer for International Business Times. *In the following viewpoint, Ghosh reports on the growing concern in Turkey over the country's falling birthrate and its demographic consequences. Many Turks have voiced worries that the high birthrate in the country's Kurdish minority will eventually lead to a Kurdish majority, which may lead to a range of potential political and social problems. One of the major issues would be the matter of Kurdish secessionism. It is thought that assimilation into the Turkish majority and providing more economic and political opportunities to the Kurdish community would solve many of these challenges.*

As you read, consider the following questions:

1. According to demographers, what is Turkey's fertility rate?
2. How long will it take for the Kurds to outnumber Turks if current trends persist, according to Ghosh?
3. What does Dr. Tino Sanandaji view as Turkey's third viable option to address the demographic imbalance?

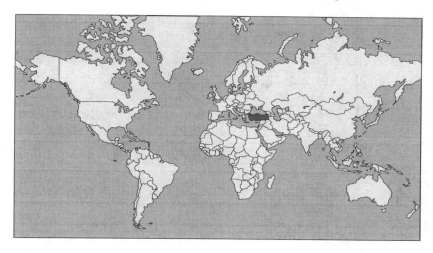

Turkey is emerging as an economic superpower in the Eastern Mediterranean and Middle East with greater influence in regional politics. Promoting itself as a "model Muslim democracy," and widely admired by other Middle Eastern nations, Turkey now faces a novel problem that Europe has long contended with: a falling birthrate.

Since the 1990s, Turkey's fertility rate has steadily declined, due to, among other factors, rising household incomes, expanded access to higher education for women and increased birth control practices.

"The use of birth control methods has increased in Turkey a lot, but that is not the only reason for the decline in population," an obstetrician named Kağan Kocatepe told *Hürriyet Daily News*, a Turkish newspaper.

"Many women want to have a successful career. That's why the maternity age has increased, as women have started giving birth to their first child in their 30s."

Indeed, Dr. Ismet Koç, a demographer at Hacettepe University in Ankara, warned that Turkey's fertility rate is now below 2.1, the replacement level, which suggests the population will eventually decline.

The fertility level in more prosperous western Turkey is now about 1.5—roughly the same as in western Europe.

The number of children produced by the average Turkish woman has plunged to two from three over just the past two decades, coincident with Turkey's rise as an economic power.

But there is a wrinkle to this whole phenomenon.

The Kurdish community of Turkey, which currently represents at least 15 percent of the population and dominates the southeastern region, has such a high birthrate, that some observers—most prominently Prime Minister Recep Tayyip Erdoğan—believe Kurds could become a majority in Turkey within two generations.

The proposed scenario is somewhat similar to the Palestinian situation in Israel, where Arabs could become the dominant ethnic group in the 'Jewish State' within 30 years or so; or the southwestern United States, where Hispanics and Mexican Americans are likely to become the majority within a few decades.

A rapidly rising Kurdish population would pose sharp problems and challenges for the Turkish state and society.

According to Turkish government statistics, the average Kurdish woman in Turkey gives birth to about four children, more than double the rate for other Turkish mothers.

Thus, Turkey is facing a demographic time bomb—Kurds, who tend to be concentrated in the country's impoverished southeast and are generally poorer and less educated, could conceivably outnumber Turks within about 30 years should present patterns persist.

Erdoğan seems to be certain this will happen.

"If we continue the existing trend, [the year] 2038 will mark disaster for us," Erdoğan warned in May 2010.

The prime minister, who has repeatedly called on Turkish couples to have three children and even suggested financially

The Kurds

The Kurds are considered the largest ethnic group in the world without their own country. Even though they live in countries that are mainly Arabic, they are not ethnically Arab and they speak a non-Arabic language called Kurdish. In the first decade of the twenty-first century, the Kurdish population living in the Middle East exceeded 25 million people, with approximately 15 million in Turkey, four million in Iraq, one million in Syria, and six and a half million in Iran. Another half million Kurds live in areas of the former Soviet Union and there are Kurdish populations in Europe and the United States. The majority of Kurds are Sunni Muslim, but there are populations of Shiite Muslim Kurds and small groups of Christian and Jewish Kurds as well.

"Kurdish Conflicts," Global Issues in
Context Online Collection, 2012.

rewarding such fecundity, once declared: "Our population is getting older. Right now we are proud of our young population, but if we don't pull these numbers up, Turkey will be in a difficult position by 2038."

Some Turkish academics scoff at Erdoğan's solutions as unrealistic.

Cem Behar, an economics professor at Istanbul's Boğaziçi University, told the *Hürriyet Daily News*: "It's clear that Turkey is going to face a decline in the growth rate of its population. Yet you cannot address such an issue by telling people to have more children."

Behar added: "There is no family policy in Turkey. And I don't think anyone is going to have more children just because [Erdoğan] told them to do so. If the government really wants to promote having more children, it needs to prepare the necessary conditions for it, such as lowering taxes for those families or strengthening preschool education."

A rapidly rising Kurdish population would pose sharp problems and challenges for the Turkish state and society.

Kurds have long faced discrimination, deprivation, even state-sponsored violence, throughout their long and epic residence in Turkey. As such, many Kurds seek a separate homeland, or at the least, autonomous self-rule in the southeast.

Kurds represent a dominant and highly contentious theme in Turkish politics.

For many years, it was, in fact, illegal for Kurds to speak their own language, use Kurdish names, play Kurdish music, etc.—part of a comprehensive attempt by Ankara to wipe out the separate ethnic identity of the Kurds. Indeed, some Turks regarded Kurds simply as 'Mountain Turks.'

The Kurdistan Workers' Party (PKK), a Marxist militant movement which Turkey, the European Union and the U.S. brand as a terrorist group, has fought for a separatist nation for decades. The PKK's periodic conflicts with the Turkish military have cost tens of thousands of lives on both sides— seemingly with no resolution in sight.

Kurds represent a dominant and highly contentious theme in Turkish politics.

Of course, many, perhaps most, Kurds in Turkey do not support the PKK and seek to assimilate with mainstream Turkish society—while retaining their distinct Kurdish culture, language and customs.

Now, with the Kurds having more babies than the Turks, will Kurds really become a majority in a country where they have long suffered abuse and deprivation? And if that were to happen, how would that affect the Kurds' status in Turkey?

International Business Times spoke with an expert on Turkey and demographics to explore this topic.

Dr. Tino Sanandaji is a PhD in public policy at the University of Chicago who does research on demographic change and its link to policy.

International Business Times: *Is the overall fertility rate in Turkey declining because the country is becoming wealthier, household incomes are rising and more women are using birth control methods?*

Dr. Tino Sanandaji: Yes, sooner or later this happens in all industrialized countries—parents prefer to have fewer children and invest more time and resources on them rather than having a large family.

The birthrate for Kurds is more than double that of Turks. Is this due to the fact that Kurds are generally poorer and less educated?

Sanandaji: Poorer, less educated and more rural. However, other factors should not be ruled out since low-income Kurdish women also have higher birthrates than low-income Turkish women.

Prime Minister Erdoğan warned that Kurds could become a majority in Turkey by 2038. Is this a realistic prediction?

Sanandaji: No, that is impossible. Demographic change is a slow process even when birthrates differ sharply, because so many generations are already born and will be around for decades.

In the 1930s, the Kurds constituted about 9 percent of the population of Turkey, and though they had higher birthrates than the Turks it still took until the 1990s until they reached the 18 percent level.

Since it takes a long time, underlying forces can change in the meanwhile. Therefore, we should be careful about extrapolating current trends into the future. Nor can demographic trends be dismissed using the equally silly argument that since demographic predictions were sometimes wrong in the past, all predictions are always wrong in the future. Plenty of predictions turned out to be accurate.

This is a sensitive topic to some. When people read that the population share of their "tribe" is shrinking there is often a primal psychological response of fear, anger or denial, and wide exaggerations in both directions.

In the event Kurds become a majority in Turkey, will that render the Kurdish nationalist and separatist movements irrelevant and moot?

Sanandaji: If history is any guide, that development would raise tensions with the Kurdish separatist movement, because they will be more likely to win a democratic or military struggle once they are the majority population.

If the Kurds are becoming more assimilated, why is this even a problem? If the Ankara government does not even classify Kurds as a separate ethnic group, why would they even care about their higher birthrates?

Sanandaji: If Kurds are slowly assimilating but growing their population share rapidly, the net effect might still be more voters with an ethnic Kurdish identity. Once Kurds realize time is working on their side, they might become less willing to abandon their national identity, anticipating that if they hold on long enough their sheer numbers will change the balance of power.

If the rate of assimilation into a national Turkish identity is sufficiently rapid, Turkey will not necessarily break apart. But Turkey will likely be a different country in many other ways if Kurds become the majority.

What, if anything, is the Turkish government doing to prevent these demographic trends?

Sanandaji: One choice is to try to stabilize the Turkish birthrate, though no country I am aware of has successfully done this in modern times.

A second alternative for the government is to convince the Kurds in Turkey to accept the Turkish national identity, making the population issue less important.

Another option is to lower the Kurdish birthrate by promoting economic development, education and women's health in Kurdish areas.

But if current trends continue for generations, Turks might eventually reach a point when they must reluctantly decide between keeping a smaller Turkish nation-state or risk becoming the minority population in a Kurdish-majority Turkey.

Iran Gives Up Birth Control Program to Boost Population

Al Arabiya

*Al Arabiya is a Saudi-owned news agency and television chan-
nel. In the following viewpoint, the author announces the plans
of Iran's religious government to dismantle existing family planning programs, which had successfully led to a drop in the
country's fertility rate through the past two decades. Many observers believe that the Iranian government's attempts to increase
the country's population is a rebuke to world sanctions imposed
over the Iranian nuclear program. The government's new push
to increase the country's fertility rate is expected to fail because
the Iranian people are hesitant to have more children during
economic and political uncertainty.*

As you read, consider the following questions:

1. What did Supreme Leader Ayatollah Ali Khamenei recently proclaim that Iran's target population should be?

2. What is Iran's current population?

3. According to the viewpoint, what percentage of Iran's
   population is under thirty-five years old?

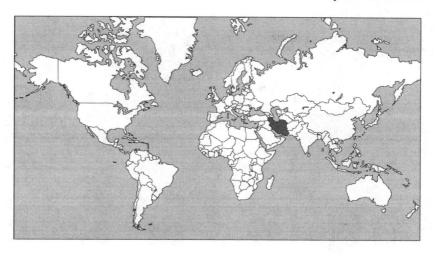

Iran has decided to get rid of its birth control program completely in a radical policy change envisioned to create a baby boom that could more than double its current population.

Supreme Leader Ayatollah Ali Khamenei recently said that the two-decade-old policy of controlled growth must end and that Iran's target is to increase its population to 150 to 200 million.

The country's current population is about 75 million, according to a recent census. Iran also topped the global list of countries facing the greatest drop in fertility rates since 1980, according to data published in 2009 by the United Nations. The reduction of births was accomplished with the help of a publicly backed initiative introduced in the early 1990s that included vasectomies, health ministry–issued contraceptives, statutory family planning advice for newlyweds and a state-owned condom factory.

Ayatollah Khamenei made a nationally televised speech, invoked by the late Ayatollah Ruhollah Khomeini, spiritual leader of the revolution, to announce that current birth control practices were no longer appropriate.

Iran Sanctions

The nuclear aspirations of Iran have kept it at odds with many other governments. Both the United Nations (UN) and the United States have imposed economic sanctions and export controls on Iran because of the country's activities in support of such groups linked to international terrorism as Lebanon's Hezbollah and to weapons proliferation. Iran has repeatedly refused to respond to international demands issued through the UN to allow oversight of its nuclear program. While willing to discuss cooperation on disarmament and nonproliferation of nuclear weapons, Iran firmly asserts that it will not abandon its nuclear activities.

"Iran," Global Issues in Context Online Collection, 2012.

"The policy of population restriction should definitely be revised and the authorities should build the culture in order to abandon the current status of one child, two children [per family]," he said.

"The figure of 150 or 200 million was once stated by the Imam [Khomeini] and that is the correct figure that we should reach," he added.

After the announcement was made, Marzieh Vahid-Dastjerdi, the health minister, told Iranian journalists that the funding had been withdrawn and that the 190 billion rials ($15.5 million) would now be used to encourage bigger families.

"The budget for the population control program has been fully eliminated and such a project no longer exists in the health ministry," she said. "The policy of population control does not exist as it did previously."

Mousa Sharififarid, an Iranian writer and pro-democracy activist, said, "the Iranian regime should rather provide prosperity for its citizens who live in miserable conditions inside the country and allow more than three million Iranian expatriates to return home than seek to increase the population."

Iranians have been asked to have more children in the past by President Mahmoud Ahmadinejad, in his bid to help Iran defeat the West.

"In Iran, more than 10 million people cannot afford to buy meat even once a month, according to a recent survey," Sharififarid said.

"It is ridiculous to see the country seeking to increase its population when many of its citizens are still trapped in deep poverty," he added.

Iranians have been asked to have more children in the past by President Mahmoud Ahmadinejad, in his bid to help Iran defeat the West. Three years ago, the president also introduced a scheme that put £600 in a bank account for every new born baby, with an additional £60 every year until they reached 18.

However, experts believe the elimination of birth control will only lead to the reluctance of couples to marry and have children in an economy full of unemployment, inflations and more recently, the effects of Western sanctions due to Iran's nuclear program.

Alireza Marandi, a former health minister and current member of the parliamentary health committee, told *Arman* newspaper that he didn't think the action taken would work at all. "Our problem is that our young people either don't marry or marry late and in Iran, as long as there is no marriage, there are no babies. And those people who marry late suffice to only one child," he said.

Ali Reza Khamesian, a columnist whose work appears in several pro-reform newspapers, told the Associated Press that the change in policy also may be an attempt to send a message to the world that Iran is not suffering from sanctions imposed over the nuclear program that the West suspects is aimed at producing weapons—something Tehran denies.

Abbas Kazemi, a doorman in a private office building, said he cannot afford to have more than two children with his salary of about $220 (4.2 million rials) a month.

"I cannot afford daily life," he said. "I have to support my wife and two children as well as my elderly parents."

More than half of Iran's population is under 35 years old. Those youth form the base of opposition groups, including the so-called Green Movement that led unprecedented street protests after President Mahmoud Ahmadinejad's disputed re-election in 2009. Some experts have said that trying to boost the numbers for upcoming generations also could feed future political dissent.

"Young people are the heart of the Arab Spring, or the Islamic Awakening as Iran calls it," said Mustafa Alani, an analyst at the Gulf Research Center based in Geneva. "Countries that haven't faced major protests during the Arab Spring still have to be mindful that the demands of the youth are still there."

Population Soars; Family Planning Efforts Remain Weak

Joanne Wanjala

Joanne Wanjala is a reporter for Global Press Institute. In the following viewpoint, she outlines plans by Kenya's National Coordinating Agency for Population and Development (NCAPD) to address cultural attitudes against the use of birth control that prevail in many parts of the country. The agency has received more funding from the Kenyan government to promote family planning services and change stereotypes and misconceptions about contraception. Programs such as this are necessary to combat the high fertility rate in the country and make progress with many of its major goals, including fighting poverty, universal primary education, food security, and a decrease in maternal and infant mortality.

As you read, consider the following questions:

1. According to Wanjala, what is the unemployment rate in Kenya?

2. According to a United States Agency for International Development (USAID) report, what will be Kenya's population in 2040 if trends continue?

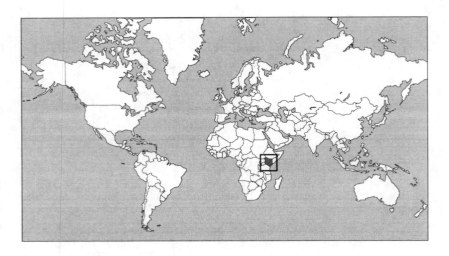

3. What is the estimated fertility rate for Kenyan women, according to the author?

Concefta Naliaka is a 48-year-old mother of 12 children.

Born in the Bungoma district in the far western region of Kenya and married at the age of 16, Naliaka says she had no knowledge of or access to birth control. She says she has always lived with the biblical adage, "multiply and fill the earth" ringing in her head.

The small grass-thatched shanty that Naliaka's large family calls home tells the tale of the economic hardship that comes from having such a large family. In Kenya—a country with a 40 percent unemployment rate—the financial realities of raising so many children are grim. Her eldest son, Robin, now 28, could not finish primary school because of financial constraints. Now, Naliaka says she struggles to provide her youngest son, Victor, who is just six, with basic needs and supplies.

Her husband, Peter Wekesa, works as a local trader at the nearest market in the town of Chwele. But his primary focus these days is the one acre of land that he farms in order to feed his large family. Wekesa says the food he grows in a year is barely enough to keep the family fed for a few months.

"My elder kids and I have to tend other people's farms in exchange for food to be able to take care of the family's food requirements," says Naliaka as she stirs the porridge that is to be the afternoon meal for the many pairs of eyes that patiently watched her.

Cultural beliefs here prevent women from using family planning methods and encourage large, ever-expanding families. "In this place, children are still regarded as a source of wealth and using any family planning is like committing murder," Naliaka says.

On familial, local and national levels, experts are concerned that Kenya's rapid population growth is hindering economic development and sustainability in the country.

Wekesa, her 52-year-old husband, earns approximately 1500 shillings per month, or $20 USD, as a trader at the local market. Naliaka says this doesn't even come close to covering the basic cost of food, shelter and clothing for a 14-member family. It's no wonder, she says, that education and health care needs go unmet.

Stereotypes Fuel Population Growth

Cultural stereotypes around contraceptives run deep here. Wekesa's neighbor and brother, Patrick Waswa, works at a local coffee factory here. He has two wives and 13 children. (Polygamy remains a factor in why many families are so large.) When asked about contraceptives, he says contraceptives are equivalent to a vasectomy, referring to them as "second knives." When asked about using condoms, "Am I a prostitute?" he quipped.

On familial, local and national levels, experts are concerned that Kenya's rapid population growth is hindering economic development and sustainability in the country.

According to the Central Bureau of Statistics and World Bank development indicators, 38 million people now reside in Kenya, a 30 percent increase in the span of 10 years. A United States Agency for International Development (USAID) poverty report released in November of 2009 warns that if this annual growth rate goes unchecked, then Kenya's population will explode to 82 million people by 2040.

Sources with the Kenya National Population and Housing Census of 2009 say that if the country is going to achieve any of its major goals—universal primary education, food security, increased health care opportunities and a reduction in maternal and infant deaths—then serious steps to control the population are necessary and overdue.

Family Planning Message Efforts to Increase

In response, the National Coordinating Agency for Population and Development (NCAPD) plans to step up family planning messaging aimed at eradicating the attitudes held by people like Wekesa and Waswa.

"The government plans to increase budgets for family planning campaigns in the next fiscal year to the level where it was in 1980s," says NCAPD's media liaison David Kinyua. He is optimistic that such a move by the government will cause fertility rates—now estimated to be 5.5 children per woman—to drop.

Dr. Boniface K'Oyugi, NCAPD chief executive officer, says it is only by controlling a country's population that development can be achieved. K'Oyugi points to Asian nations that limit procreation in order to meet development milestones.

Many on the ground say they are skeptical that messaging alone will change deep-seated beliefs and ancient cultural practices that prize large families.

Madagascar: Peer Pressure to Stop Teen Pregnancy

Integrated Regional Information Networks (IRIN)

Integrated Regional Information Networks (IRIN) is a news agency that focuses on humanitarian subjects in developing and troubled regions. In the following viewpoint, the author discusses the efforts in Madagascar to address high teenage pregnancy rates. The government believes that the initiative is necessary because of the severe medical problems many girls face after childbirth and the high rates of infant and maternal mortality. International authorities have joined the effort, working to change cultural attitudes about contraception; opening new clinics that offer women's health and contraceptive services; and training young volunteers to teach their peers about HIV, sexually transmitted diseases (STDs), and birth control.

As you read, consider the following questions:

1. According to the United Nations Population Fund, how many mothers in Madagascar die during or soon after delivery?

2. How many women does the United Nations Population Fund estimate experience medical problems after delivery?

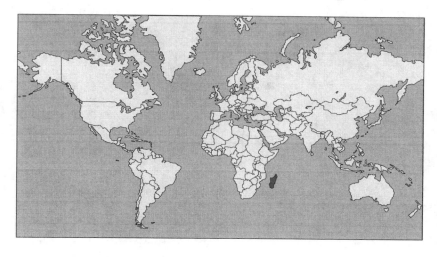

3. For how much money does the author report that families in Madagascar are selling their daughters?

Daughters as young as 12 in the villages surrounding Antsohihy, the capital of the Sofia region, in Madagascar's remote, traditional north, often suffer the harmful consequences of falling pregnant and giving birth too young when parents accept zebus (cattle) or cash as a dowry.

Noeline Razafindradera, 16, wishes she had listened to the warnings of her mother and her teachers. Instead, she went out with one of the boys she met at school and became pregnant. After going into labour, she waited two days before leaving her village of Ambongabe and then travelled two more days by ox cart to reach the Baptist Good Hope Hospital in the town of Mandritsara. By then, the baby was dead and it had to be removed.

Three months later, Razafindradera is back at the hospital for a procedure to repair an obstetric fistula—a severe medical condition in which a hole (fistula) develops between the bladder and the vagina, or between the rectum and the vagina— caused by difficult delivery. The surgeon performs the operation for a subsidized price of 10,000 ariary (US$5 dollars).

"Many young girls have this problem," said hospital director and surgeon Adrien Ralimiarison. "Girls as young as 13 become pregnant. The pelvis of the girl is too small, so during delivery the head of the baby gets stuck. As it takes a long time to reach a hospital, the bladder can then erupt. After the delivery, these girls are often rejected because of the smell of leaking urine and the additional expense of soap and pads. In some villages, people even believe that these women are evil. Depression often follows."

This is confirmed by his next patient, Rasoanirina, 21, who also developed the condition after a protracted labour and a three-day journey to the hospital from her village. "People reject you, they don't want to stay near you because of the smell," she said.

At the Good Hope Hospital, a relative haven in the midst of a neglected and inadequate health sector, Yolande Zafindraivo is the only gynaecologist in this region of over 1 million inhabitants. "There are no doctors or trained midwives in the villages, so people deliver with the help of the village matron, the elder woman of the village who has knowledge of traditional medicine," she told IRIN. "It's dangerous—the matrons give the girls traditional herbs to induce the baby, [but] these are very strong and can cause a shock reaction in the body."

Zafindraivo concentrates on saving the mothers, and says she succeeds most of the time. Nonetheless, figures from the UN Population Fund (UNFPA) reveal that the Sofia region has one of the highest maternal death rates in the country, with 1 in every 10 mothers dying during childbirth.

Nationwide, 3,750 mothers and 16,500 babies die each year during or soon after delivery. Another 75,000 women experience medical problems as a result of childbirth, and an estimated 40 percent of these women receive insufficient care.

"These are the official hospital and health clinic figures. We don't know how many die at home with the matrons,"

Obstetric Fistula

Each year between 50,000 to 100,000 women worldwide are affected by obstetric fistula, a hole in the birth canal. The development of obstetric fistula is directly linked to one of the major causes of maternal mortality: obstructed labour.

Women who experience obstetric fistula suffer constant incontinence, shame, social segregation and health problems. It is estimated that more than 2 million young women live with untreated obstetric fistula in Asia and sub-Saharan Africa.

Obstetric fistula is preventable; it can largely be avoided by:

- delaying the age of first pregnancy;

- the cessation of harmful traditional practices; and

- timely access to obstetric care.

"10 Facts on Obstetric Fistula,"
World Health Organization, March 2010.

said Zafindraivo. "Often people prefer the matrons, as they think hospitals are expensive and they know these women."

Hospitals in the region, as well as UNFPA, are training community health workers and matrons to avoid delays in getting women in need of care during childbirth to a hospital. Dr Jean Francois Xavier of UNFPA said the goal was to reduce the three kinds of delay: leaving home, reaching a hospital, and finding care once they arrive.

Community Training

"We try to shorten all this lost time by building capacity in the community," he said. "This includes training for the matrons, who are taught that a woman in labour should not see the sun rise twice. After 24 hours, she needs to be sent on to a health clinic or hospital. We also support the network of clinics and maternity wards, where women can deliver for free. There we train community health workers and provide kits for delivery and for caesarean sections."

[The United Nations Population Fund] is trying to reach more young people with birth control.

This system worked in the case of Volasaina Ratongarizafy, 19, who is recovering from a caesarean section after coming by car from Port Berger, 122km to the south of Antsohihy. The midwife sent Ratongarizafy to the hospital after she had been in labour for two days, and she waited only an hour to be operated on.

UNFPA is trying to reach more young people with birth control. Madeleine Razanajafy, a health worker at the maternity clinic in Antsohihy, said girls rarely used birth control once they marry. "Often, the husbands don't want their wives to use birth control . . . [they think] it opens the way to promiscuity [for the wives]," she said.

Reaching girls before they become sexually active is also not easy because many leave school early, said Xavier. "After they have a baby, they give the child to the grandparents to raise—this problem puts pressure on society everywhere."

In an effort to overcome some of the obstacles, UNFPA has built a special clinic for young people on the premises of the maternity clinic in Antsohihy, where it supplies birth control options that last several months, such as hormone patches, injections or intrauterine devices (IUDs).

Local NGOs, like Vilavila, are also training young volunteers to talk to their peers about HIV, sexually transmitted infections (STIs), and birth control, while village elders lead group discussions with parents to try to counter the custom of trading young girls for cows or money.

"These parents are poor, so it's hard for them to refuse— sometimes they are offered as much as 2 million ariary ($1,000)," said Vilavila director Piantoni Rabarison. "We show movies and have discussions with them. Often, they admit they hadn't thought about the effect their actions could have on the young girls."

Local [nongovernmental organizations] . . . are also training young volunteers to talk to their peers about HIV, sexually transmitted infections (STIs), and birth control.

At the Good Hope Hospital, surgeon Ralimiarison asks his patients to reach out to other girls through a radio programme. "I can say many things, and I regularly do, but these girls are my ambassadors. They can tell their peers to be careful, to make sure that they don't fall pregnant."

Periodical and Internet Sources Bibliography

The following articles have been selected to supplement the diverse views presented in this chapter.

Mohammad Mohiuddin Abdullah	"Controlling the Population Boom," *Daily Star* (Bangladesh), January 7, 2013.
Edith Fortunate and Aggrey Mutambo	"Birth Control Takes Centre Stage as World Population Hits 7 Billion," *Daily Nation* (Kenya), October 31, 2011.
Mireya Navarro	"Breaking a Long Silence on Population Control," *New York Times*, October 31, 2011.
Elisabeth Rosenthal	"Nigeria Tested by Rapid Rise in Population," *New York Times*, April 14, 2012.
Farzaneh Roudi	"Iran Is Reversing Its Population Policy," Wilson Center, August 2012. http://www.wilson center.org/publication/iran-reversing-its -population-policy.
Robert Tait	"Iran Scraps State-Sponsored Birth Control Policy," *Telegraph*, August 3, 2012.
Toronto Star	"World's Population Hits Seven Billion; Challenges Abound, Notably in Asia, Africa," October 16, 2011.
USA Today	"Iran Urges Baby Boom, Slashes Birth-Control Programs," July 29, 2012.
Kenneth R. Weiss	"Fertility Rates Fall, but Global Population Explosion Goes On," *Los Angeles Times*, July 22, 2012.
Robert Zubrin	"China's Population-Control Holocaust," *Washington Times*, May 21, 2012.

GLOBALVIEWPOINTS

CHAPTER 2

Politics and Birth Control

Rick Santorum and the Sexual Counter-Revolution

Laurie Penny

Laurie Penny is a reporter and columnist for the New States-man. *In the following viewpoint, she views the American contro-versy over the birth control mandate to be part of a larger back-lash against the sexual revolution, which allowed women greater control over their own sexuality and reproductive freedom. Penny notes that Republicans perceive the issue of insurance coverage for contraception to be one of religious freedom and hope to capitalize on it in the 2012 election—although public opinion seems to be against them. A controversy over abortion rights and sexual health has also erupted in Britain, where conservative politicians have been attacking access to abortion and sexual education.*

As you read, consider the following questions:

1. What American human rights activist was arrested in February 1916 for distributing birth control pamphlets in New York City?

2. According to a *New York Times* poll, what percentage of Catholic voters support requiring employee health care plans to cover the cost of birth control?

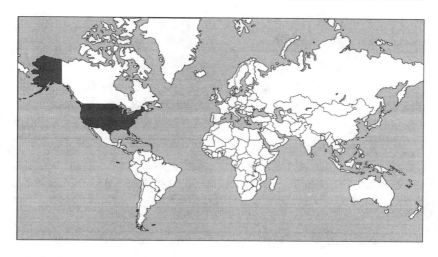

3. What does Penny identify as the first step in a technological revolution that liberated women from functional
dependence on men?

Almost a century ago this month, women's rights activist
Emma Goldman was arrested in New York for distributing "obscene, lewd, or lascivious articles". What she was doing
was handing out pamphlets about birth control, with the aim
of freeing women sexually and socially from the burden of
unwanted pregnancy, and she got a spell in a prison work-
house for her trouble.

Walk around Lower Manhattan today, as I did this morning, and you'd think that history had vindicated Goldman's
long campaign for sexual freedom.

Pop songs promising a catalogue of horizontal delights
pump out of the doorways of shops selling dildos and cheap
knickers in the early mornings. Men hold hands with their
husbands in SoHo. Wall Street workers in skirt suits jostle on
the subway with excited teenagers in tiny shorts defying their
parents and the winter chill.

Everywhere, on billboards and bus stops and hoardings a
hundred feet high, images of female sexual availability bulge

and shine and flutter their perfect airbrushed eyelashes. Thighs glisten, legs spread and giant red lips open wetly for the latest low-calorie yoghurt. Surely, you'd think, this is a sweaty shangri-la of erotic liberty. Surely this is one place where the sexual revolution of the 1960s was allowed to reach its logical conclusion.

In 2012, the morality of hormonal birth control is now a serious hot-button issue in the Republican presidential race.

Step into any coffee shop or diner that carries the rolling news, however, and you'll find that in the land of the free not everything is as free as it seems. Over the past few weeks, right-wing politicians have launched an all-out assault on women's sexual and reproductive freedom and LGBT rights, attacking not just gay marriage and abortion but contraception, too.

In 2012, the morality of hormonal birth control is now a serious hot-button issue in the Republican presidential race. Last week, not a single woman was allowed to testify before a Washington hearing on reproductive rights and "religious freedom"—which includes allowing bosses to deny their female employees contraceptive health coverage on moral grounds.

Meanwhile, the state of Virginia debated whether or not to force every women seeking an abortion to submit to vaginal probing with an ultrasound device, a policy that campaigners called "state-sponsored rape"—one state representative commented that he couldn't see what the problem was, as these women had already consented to being penetrated when they got pregnant.

As panels of terrifying old men gather on national television to debate whether and how far women should be punished for having sex outside marriage one could be forgiven

"YOU HAVE A VISITOR AND...OH!...OH!... HE LOOKS ANGRY!"

for thinking that American politics had temporarily been scripted by Margaret Atwood. As the recession crunches down, the country is awash with anti-erotic, anti-queer, anti-woman rhetoric that goes beyond 'culture war' into the territory of sexual counter-revolution.

The Republicans know that contraception in particular is a losing issue for them—a *New York Times* poll found that two-thirds of voters, including 67 per cent of Catholics, support requiring employee health care plans to cover the cost of birth control, and Obama is up ten points with women from August—but they can't help themselves. One whiff of uncontrolled pudenda and they start scrapping like house dogs who have been sprayed with pheromones, which makes for such classic TV moments as candidate Newt Gingrich, currently America's most famous serial adulterer, seriously participating in a debate about sexual continence.

To call this backlash a culture war would be to imply that more than one side is fighting.

This is far from the case. Compared to pageant of homophobic and misogynist pants-wetting going on on the American right, all the Democrats need to do to make themselves look like a sane and useful political outfit is to sit back and watch the Republicans engage in auto-erotic asphyxiation.

Americans have short memories, particularly in election years, and most seem to have forgotten that it is barely two months since President Obama stepped in to restrict the sale of the morning-after pill to girls under 17—a move seemingly designed to reassure the increasingly suspicious, sexist American centre-right that he hates sexual freedom a little bit, too. Just not as much as those crazy Republicans.

Curiously enough, precisely the same arguments seem to be at play when British conservatives attack abortion rights and sexual health—they might be gradually reintroducing fear of female sexuality into mainstream public life, but at least they're not as bad as those crazy Americans. Meanwhile, the public conversation about women's rights and sexual freedom creeps back, inch by inch, towards conservative censoriousness.

It's worth reminding ourselves what birth control and abortion actually mean in political terms.

This new sexual counter-revolution is bigger than America. The rhetoric of god, marriage, morality and little girls learning to keep their legs closed has crossed the pond with all the tooth-aching tenacity of a Katy Perry song. Last week, we had Baroness Warsi going to the Vatican to announce that Europe needs to be more 'confident in its Christianity'.

This week, it's a campaign by the *Telegraph* to remind women, their doctors and the government that abortions are not available 'on demand', a move that follows two years of attacks on sex education and the legal right to choose in parliament. Just like in the United States, the effect of this mission creep of legislative misogyny is to chip away at public support for women's rights to control our bodies and our destinies.

It's worth reminding ourselves what birth control and abortion actually mean in political terms. The hormonal birth control pill was the first step in a technological revolution that, within living memory, liberated one-half of the human race from functional dependency on the other. With legal abortion as the other side of the equation should birth control fail, women can finally be the mistresses of our own reproductive systems, rather than the slaves of it.

We can choose when, if and how many children we want, we can be sexually active without fear of pregnancy, and we can participate, at least in theory, in every area of public and professional life—we can have, in short, all the advantages that men have always enjoyed through accident of biology.

Pro-choice campaigners speak of a woman's right to "control her own body", rather than have it controlled for her by her husband, the church or the state, as if that right were a social given rather than something that our mothers and grandmothers fought and went to prison to win.

When conservative headbangers like Rick Santorum complain that birth control encourages women and girls to have sex outside marriage, the appropriate response should be "yes, and?". Of course we want to have sex outside marriage without fear of social or economic punishment. Of course we want to control our fertility and, with it, our future.

These are precisely the technological advances that make real equality a possibility, and they are precisely the advances that players in the big boys' throwback club of modern politics wish to curtail when they complain of "moral decline" in public life.

The sexual counter-revolution is all about control. It's about control of women, control of desire, and control of political space at a time when elected representatives have nothing to offer voters beyond sops to our most fearful prejudices. As for those dirty billboards, they are part of the equation. A culture of objectification is part of managing and monetising the social fact of desire.

Anglo-American culture has never had a problem with sex as long as it is carefully managed—as long as it is enjoyed only by straight men and endured by women, guiltily, in the dark.

China's One Child Policy: Two Cases

Jing Zhang

Jing Zhang is president of Women's Rights in China. In the following viewpoint, she reviews the two tragic cases of Cao Ruyi and Feng Jianmei as examples of the terrible abuses perpetrated on men and women who violate China's strict birth planning system. One of the women endured near-forced abortion and the other forced abortion at the hands of the Chinese government. Zhang argues that women have no reproductive rights in China. Moreover, Americans need to be aware of the suffering endured by Chinese women and to condemn forced abortion and sterilization in China.

As you read, consider the following questions:

1. How much did the Family Planning Commision fine Cao Ruyi for her pregnancy?

2. How many months pregnant was Feng Jianmei when her pregnancy was forcibly aborted?

3. According to Zhang, what do Americans need to stop funding, and why?

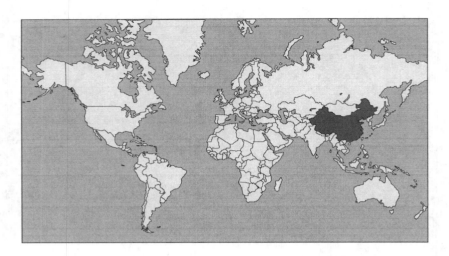

During these last few weeks, media reports about Chen Guangcheng's arrival in New York and China's brutal one-child policy continue to raise awareness in the United States about a real war on women. China's one-child policy is supported by the UN and is sponsored by U.S. tax dollars through UNFPA. In an election year, we need to educate our elected officials and American citizens about why this real war against women must end. Consider these two cases.

Cao Ruyi Returns Home After Five-Day Detention, Still Ordered to Undergo Abortion

After several days of domestic and international media and public pressure, Cao Ruyi, a pregnant woman who had been detained for five days by Hongshan District, Changsha Family Planning Commission, was allowed to return home. However, China's government continues to be a threat to forcibly terminate her pregnancy.

Around 9 o'clock on June 10, after performing an ultrasound exam on Cao Ruyi in the Hunan Province Women and Children's Hospital, Family Planning officials planned to detain her at the Changsha County Women and Children's Hospital. Despite heavy coercion, Cao resisted, and remained determined to let her child live. Family Planning officials brought her to one of three permanently rented rooms in the Beifu Hotel. They forced her to sign the Order to Terminate Pregnancy within Set Time, with the stipulation that she must have an abortion before October 16. Past that date, she would be subject to the fine of the "end of pregnancy collateral." Cao signed the document solely because of her utter exhaustion. She returned home at noon accompanied by a cousin and a WRIC volunteer.

Cao Ruyi told the WRIC volunteer that the "collateral" was set by the Family Planning Commission at between 2,000 to 10,000 yuan. The fine imposed on her was 10,000 yuan, just for the pregnancy. If she did not pay the fine in time, the birth of the child would mean fines of over 100,000 yuan. Cao was determined to have the child. Cao was unemployed. Her husband had to support the whole family including Cao's mother-in-law. The financial situation of the family was difficult. Paying the fines would be impossible.

Because Feng Jianmei is poor and her family is unable to pay the fine of 40,000 yuan that was imposed on her, Family Planning officials forcibly aborted Jianmei.

Sadder yet is that WRIC has received information that Cao Ruyi has been quietly threatened by a local Family Planning officer, Yan Zhang, who told Cao that she has "friends in the military." Cao and her family are living in fear of what acts of revenge the government may take against them. They are also worried about the prenatal and perinatal care that may or may not be available.

WRIC has found a place where Cao and her husband can live in safety from government officials until her child is born. She remains in hiding with her husband. If her husband were

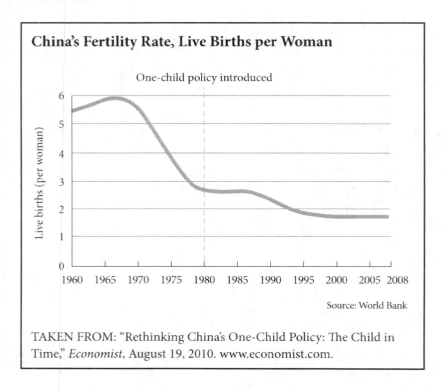

China's Fertility Rate, Live Births per Woman

One-child policy introduced

Live births (per woman)

6
5
4
3
2
1
0

1960 1965 1970 1975 1980 1985 1990 1995 2000 2005 2008

Source: World Bank

TAKEN FROM: "Rethinking China's One-Child Policy: The Child in Time," *Economist*, August 19, 2010. www.economist.com.

not in hiding, government officials would likely capture him and torture him until he agreed to help get his wife aborted.

Feng Jianmei Forcibly Aborted at Seven Months

Feng Jianmei was 7 months pregnant with her second daughter. Because Feng Jianmei is poor and her family is unable to pay the fine of 40,000 yuan that was imposed on her, Family Planning officials forcibly aborted Jianmei. On June 2, while her husband, Deng Jiyuan, was at work, Feng Jianmei fought against Family Planning officials as they tried to force her into a car. She was beaten and dragged into the vehicle, and forcibly admitted into a hospital where labor was induced. The body of her aborted daughter was savagely left next to her on her bed. [Editor's note: A picture of this scene was included with this submission, but is too graphic to be published.]

Government officials in China remain outraged that stories and photos of this case have been released to the public, but families in China are all too familiar with the cruelties that precede and follow many abortions in China.

Feng Jianmei remains under medical treatment in Ankang City, Zhenping County, Zengjia Town, Yupin village. Her husband remains tormented because his family's life has been shattered.

China's Procurator officials went to the home of Deng Jiyuan to demand answers about how the photo was made available to the media, and to forbid them to speak to the media.

Crimes Against Humanity

Women in China have no reproductive rights. No permit, no pregnancy. There is no right for women to give birth. Those are the rules. Many Americans believe that those involved in should be prosecuted crimes against humanity.

Unlike Vice President Biden, we all need to second-guess China's one-child policy, especially since China has no plans to end this policy for at least another generation. Aside from the personal human suffering each aborted woman must endure, Americans need to know about the suffering that exists for the spouses and parents and most families in China who can no longer have brothers and sisters and will never be aunts and uncles.

As Americans, we need to appeal to our president and to all of the members of Congress, especially during this election year, to condemn forced abortion, forced sterilization, and coerced family planning in China. We need to appeal to American taxpayers to stop funding UNFPA with millions and millions of U.S. dollars that sponsor these programs.

Nigeria Urges Family Planning: Why Legislation Would Be a Bad Idea

Jacey Fortin

Jacey Fortin is a reporter for the International Business Times. *In the following viewpoint, she discusses the Nigerian government's plans to introduce new birth control legislation, which was announced by President Goodluck Jonathan. Jonathan assured Nigerians that the anticipated legislation would take into account religious sensibilities but would strive to address the problem of the country's high fertility rate. The aim of the legislation would be to encourage Nigerians to have the number of children that they can afford and manage.*

As you read, consider the following questions:

1. According to the UN, how big can the population of Nigeria be by 2100?
2. According to Fortin, what is the fertility rate for Nigeria?
3. Fertility rates go hand in hand with what, in Fortin's opinion?

On Wednesday, Nigerian president Goodluck Jonathan said that families need to use planning and birth control to cut back on the number of children they have.

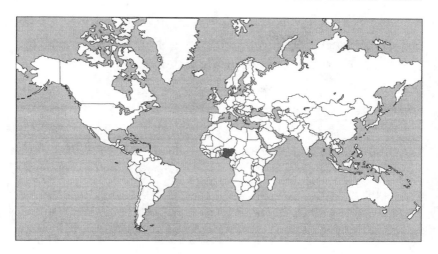

The key thing is how you will ... begin to encourage Nigerians to have the number of children they can manage, before government comes up with clear policies and guidelines, he said, according to a Nigerian newspaper.

First and foremost is the personal consciousness that people should get the families they can manage.

More family planning would undoubtedly have a positive effect in Nigeria, where overpopulation is a definite problem. This most populous country in Africa, and the seventh most populated country on earth, has more than 170 million people. That exceeds the population of Russia, and it's more than twice the population of Germany.

According to some estimates from the UN, Nigeria's population could reach a whopping 730 million by the year 2100. This would put Nigeria in third place worldwide, trailing China, which has over 10 times Nigeria's land mass, and India, which has over three times the land mass.

A fertility rate of 5.38 percent—the 13th highest on earth—is bad news for a country where over 60 percent of the population lives in absolute poverty. And these poverty rates are rising.

So Jonathan's call for smaller families is warranted—in fact, such statements are nothing new. For years, Nigeria has struggled to find ways to stem the rapid growth of its population.

In 2011, the government spent about $3 million on contraceptive and antenatal care, according to IRIN news. This was augmented by assistance from international donors and nongovernmental organizations. In April of last year, the government began providing condoms and other contraceptives for free at hospitals. Demand for these products is slowly increasing, and more women seek training on the prevention of unwanted pregnancies.

But taboos still exist. Many religious leaders argue that allowing the use of contraceptives is akin to promoting promiscuity. And abortion remains illegal in Nigeria, unless a mother's life is endangered by her pregnancy.

Jonathan said he is aware that such issues are very sensitive.

Both Christians and Muslims, and even traditionalist and all the other religions, believe that children are God's gifts to man, he said. So it is difficult for you to tell any Nigerian to [limit the number of] their children because they are gifts of God, and it is not expected to reject God's gifts.

He also mentioned uneducated people in particular were having too many children.

Here, Jonathan touched on one of Nigeria's underlying problems. Poverty and lack of education are endemic to the West African country, but Nigeria is not demographically homogenous—some areas have it worse than others.

Northern regions, whose inhabitants are mostly Muslims, have much higher rates of poverty. In northern states, the rates reach up to 86 percent, according to a government re-

Poverty in Nigeria

In 2012, the National Bureau of Statistics released a report that showed the percentage of Nigerians living in "absolute poverty" had risen from 54.7 percent in 2004 to 60.9 percent in 2010. This represented a jump from 68.7 million people in poverty in 2004 to an estimated 112.4 million in 2010. Poverty levels are higher in the northern regions of the country, with rates of about 77.7 percent in the northwest and 76.3 percent in the northeast. The northwest state of Sokoto had the highest 2012 poverty level in the country, at 86.4 percent. In the southwest, the poverty rate was estimated at 59.1 percent. According to the results of a 2010 survey, nearly 94 percent of respondents considered themselves to be poor, in comparison to 75.5 percent of respondents who claimed poverty in a 2004 survey.

"Nigeria," Global Issues in Context Online Collection, 2012.

port released this year. The mostly Christian southern regions, on the other hand, have much lower rates of poverty; in the southwest, it's at 59 percent.

It is true that legislation to bring down fertility rates, if successful, would help to stem population growth and combat poverty.

High fertility rates go hand in hand with poverty and a lack of education, so Jonathan was correct to say that less educated families are more likely to have children they cannot support. But regional differences make the statement politically thorny—as if debates over family planning and contraception weren't sensitive enough.

The stickiest point was Jonathan's suggestion that he may move beyond mere recommendations and, in the future, consider implementing actual policies to keep birthrates down. Such legislation could amount to a risky provocation—its effects would be felt most strongly in northern regions, due to the endemic poverty and higher fertility rates there. This could exacerbate north-south divisions, in addition to stirring up religious objections.

It is true that legislation to bring down fertility rates, if successful, would help to stem population growth and combat poverty. But the converse is true as well: Ameliorating poverty, especially if that involves improving health care and universal access to education, would help to bring down fertility rates. And since moving in that direction is less controversial—and, more importantly, unlikely to incite any increase in religiously motivated clashes—it would be judicious to use legislation to stem population growth from that angle instead. Family planning should be left to public awareness campaigns, not policies.

Unfortunately, the fight against poverty in Nigeria has so far been a serious failure. The central government is plagued by high levels of corruption, and nearly all Nigerians deplore its lack of efficiency. It is for this reason that the country's crude oil revenues, which have helped the sub-Saharan country achieve an impressive GDP of about $250 billion, have not resulted in a decrease in poverty levels.

But the fact remains that Nigeria does have the resources to bring assistance to the people who need it most. With money the government already makes, public awareness campaigns could be strengthened, women's health care programs could be funded, and a better public education system could be implemented.

If revenues could have been found to fund legislation to prevent large families, there's hope that it could also be found to combat the poverty-related problems that lead to high fertility rates in the first place—and that's the safer bet.

Uganda Finds Birth Control to Be a Challenging Political Issue

Madeleine Bunting

Madeleine Bunting is a columnist for the Guardian. *In the following viewpoint, she finds that the issue of birth control is a controversial one in Uganda, where the birthrate is high and cultural attitudes are negative toward the concept of family planning. Bunting reports that the president of Uganda encourages the high fertility rate for political reasons, although population growth perpetuates terrible poverty in the country as well as high child mortality rates, low levels of education, and poor health. She argues that finding ways to empower women in Uganda is essential to lowering the birthrate. To accomplish this, the Ugandan government should expand access to education for girls, improve job opportunities for women, and offer better family planning services in urban and rural areas.*

As you read, consider the following questions:

1. According to the author, what is the total population of Uganda?
2. How many children is it not uncommon for women to have in Ugandan villages, according to Bunting?

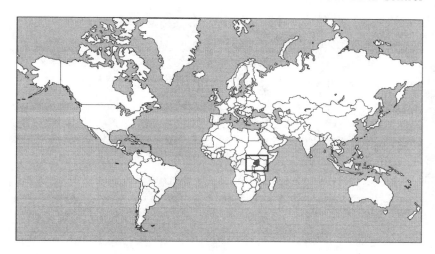

3. How many Ugandan women does Bunting report die in botched illegal abortions every year?

Birth control is one of the most sensitive and difficult issues in Uganda. The country has one of the highest population growth rates in Africa with an average of well over five children per woman. The total population is now nearing 30 million and at the current rate of growth could double, even quadruple, in a matter of decades.

I've noticed that many comments on blogs pick up on this issue; for example, [one blogger] made a comment on this issue, arguing that Uganda, "has no hope unless it can get this under control". It's a view for which Professor Teddy Brett has some sympathy.

More children often means poorer health and contributes to child mortality.

Poverty and Birthrate

A longtime observer and academic on Uganda, Brett notes that no country has managed to substantially reduce poverty with birthrates of that order. Uganda's considerable economic growth rates in recent years are swallowed up by the many new mouths which need feeding and the millions of youngsters needing jobs. Unemployment cannot be substantially reduced with Uganda's level of population growth rate.

But the government has no time for this kind of analysis. President Yoweri Museveni is very dismissive of Western attitudes on this subject. He points out that Uganda has roughly the same landmass as the UK [United Kingdom] and that the UK's population is double that of Uganda. The UK went through a population explosion in the early nineteenth century during industrialisation so why can't Uganda also increase its population, he argues.

Political Implications

What must be operating in Museveni's mind is the wider regional politics. Uganda has unstable neighbours on almost all sides—civil wars in Sudan and Congo, instability now in Kenya, while the peace in Rwanda is fragile ever since the horrific massacres of 1994. Population strength must be a consideration in his analysis of how to ensure that Uganda is able to maintain its own influence and weight in the affairs of the region. He encourages mothers to keep on having children.

The Situation for Women

His policy makes those interested in improving the health of women and children despair. It is not uncommon for women in the villages to have ten or more children; their bodies are worn out from childbearing by the time they reach their mid-thirties. Yet it is women who do most of the agriculture on which the family depends for food, so her strength is critical to the chances children have of a full stomach. The family resources get stretched thinly over large numbers of children—there is less money for medicines or costs of schooling. More children often means poorer health and contributes to child mortality.

A Public Relations Campaign Gone Wrong

The nongovernmental organisations [NGOs] are clearly trying to promote child spacing and fewer children. In the urban areas in Mbale, Jinja and Kampala, there are huge billboards showing happy couples with just two children. But sometimes the message simply goes straight over people's heads.

One Ugandan explained how an advertising campaign backfired. It juxtaposed two images: one was of a father loaded down with lots of children, the other showed the same man with just two children getting into a smart new car. The message seemed obvious: have fewer children and you will be better off. But Ugandans read it the other way: look at the lucky man with all those children and look at that poor man with only a car!

This is at the core of the issue. It is not Museveni who makes Ugandan families have so many children, nor is it the Catholic Church (which is very powerful in some areas of the country); there is a deeply embedded attitude that having a lot of children is a good thing. In part it is pragmatic—children look after you when you are old, and since many children die, you need plenty to ensure a few outlive you. But it is more than that. Producing children is considered absolutely essential to your identity.

The Power of Cultural Attitudes

One Ugandan in Katine helped explain it to me. He is one of seventeen children in a family in which his father had several wives. That was too many, he said, so he was going to have only five which he believed was a modest number. When I expressed some surprise, he insisted he couldn't have fewer, otherwise people would ask what on earth were he and his wife doing. Was he a real man? Was she a real woman? Children are a vital part of your identity.

This is partly what makes it so difficult when a woman does want to control her fertility. Often her husband is hostile to any form of birth control and she has to do it secretly. Given the government's stance, access to family planning does not feature significantly in the state health service. Abortion is illegal in Uganda and it is estimated that 1,000 women die every year in botched illegal terminations. The odds are stacked against a woman getting the help she needs to reduce her pregnancies.

It is interesting how many comments on articles about Katine have raised this issue. Some Westerners see this as a very clear-cut issue: have fewer babies and then you will be better off. But the reality is so different: very few women have a choice to take that course.

Empowering Women

Reducing fertility was achieved in the West over the course of a century of female education, national family planning services and the opening up of job opportunities for women. These three elements were crucial and all three are inadequate in Uganda.

This is why some NGOs argue that the single biggest thing you can do to effect change in the country is to educate women. The best chance of reducing fertility and spacing families is when a woman has some status, the confidence to assert herself so that she can look after her own well-being and that of her children.

The next time someone posts a comment about birth control, perhaps they ought to put their hand in their pocket to pay for the female education which could bring that outcome about?

Canada Does Not Prioritize Birth Control on Its Health Agenda

Brigitte Noël

Brigitte Noël is a journalist. In the following viewpoint, she suggests that the Canadian health care system relies too much on hormonal contraception at the expense of nonhormonal forms of birth control and research into new options. Noël contends that birth control pills, the most common form of contraception in Canada, are heavily marketed across North America and therefore are commonly prescribed to young women by physicians. As a result, nonhormonal methods are often overlooked, leading to less information and a reduced supply. She argues that nonhormonal methods should be more accepted and more widely discussed in Canada.

As you read, consider the following questions:

1. According to a 2009 United Nations report, what is the world's most popular form of reversible birth control?
2. How much does the author report that the Canadian Institutes of Health Research has spent on birth control–related research since 2008?

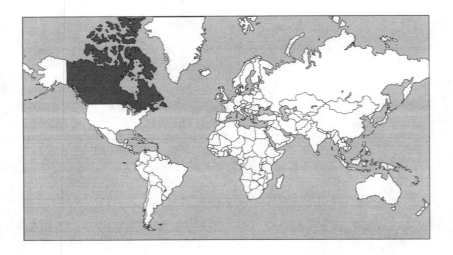

3. What are some of the side effects of hormonal contraception, according to Noël?

Sitting up on the examination table, I can hear my sterile paper gown crinkling with every movement. The gynecologist sits a few feet away, looking up at me, and I feel like a stage performer as I explain the reason for my visit. "I've tried and hated almost every type of hormonal birth control," I tell her. "I want to know about non-hormonal options." She nods when I reveal I'm in a long-term, monogamous relationship; she tenses up when I say I'm interested in an IUD [intrauterine device] or a diaphragm.

My request was uncommon. Hormonal contraception is the unequivocal norm for most young Canadian women, and research for other options is virtually nonexistent in this country. Birth control is low on the health agenda, and this oversight is putting Canadian women at risk.

Personal Experience

In the last decade, I've sampled nearly ten kinds of hormonal contraception. By the age of 19, I had tried five different types of oral contraceptive. Puberty came with a prescription for the pill to help control heavy periods. In university, hormonal contraception threw me into an emotional frenzy. Going from the pill to the Depo-Provera injection to the NuvaRing, I experienced symptoms that included an obsession with my weight, loss of my sex drive and intense mood swings. As a responsible young adult in a long-term relationship, I was a good candidate for a vaginal barrier method or an intrauterine device (IUD), but I was unaware of those options and they were never mentioned. Campus physicians continued to advocate hormonal methods, convinced they could find "the right match." Still, my body was completely uncooperative. I assumed I was the problem.

My latest attempt, a consultation with a gyno, earned me a prescription for a diaphragm. After trying more than a dozen pharmacies, I discovered that diaphragms are nearly nonexistent in Canada. A call to the manufacturer revealed that in 2010, less than 100 devices were distributed across the country.

Advancement in non-hormonal birth control is not a popular field of research and statistics show Canadians are particularly unaware.

Finally turning online, research led me to the FemCap, a highly recommended new version of the cervical cap. An American product, it's said to be comfortable, reusable, purchasable online and most importantly, hormone free. I included the recommended organic spermicide with my order, because it's not available in Canadian pharmacies.

When my gadget came in the mail, my boyfriend and I watched the unintentionally hilarious instructional video, which features a real vagina and animated sperm whose mission to fertilize is thwarted by the FemCap. To be sure, I ran the device by my family doctor. She'd never even heard of it,

What Is Intrauterine Contraception?

Intrauterine contraception, or IUC (sometimes referred to as intrauterine device or IUD), is a small T-shaped device made of soft, flexible plastic. Two types are available in the U.S.:

- ParaGard intrauterine copper contraceptive: Also known as the Copper T IUD, it is made with copper and plastic and prevents pregnancy by blocking sperm from meeting with and fertilizing an egg.

- Mirena intrauterine system (IUS): Like the ParaGard, the Mirena IUS works by stopping sperm from meeting with and fertilizing an egg. The Mirena IUS also prevents pregnancy by releasing a small amount of progestin (a hormone found in birth control pills) that keeps the ovaries from releasing an egg. Hormones are chemicals that control how different parts of your body work.

"Intrauterine Contraception (IUD) Fact Sheet,"
US Department of Health and Human Services, 2012.

but she was enthusiastic. After giving it her seal of approval, she asked to keep the instructional pamphlets I brought in.

Non-Hormonal Forms of Birth Control

Advancement in non-hormonal birth control is not a popular field of research and statistics show Canadians are particularly unaware. The United Nations 2009 report on contraceptive use says the world's most popular form of reversible birth control is the IUD. This is the method of choice for 14 per cent of the world's women. While the report shows the pill is the most popular option for most developed countries, on the global scale only nine per cent of women rely on it. In Canada, one in every five women uses oral contraceptives. The condom is second in popularity with 15 per cent, followed by traditional techniques like the rhythm method at nine per cent. The IUD and vaginal barrier methods (including the diaphragm and the FemCap) are each used by only one per cent of women. In contrast, a whopping 13.5 per cent of European women report using an IUD and 14 per cent rely on natural family planning.

So why are Canadian women so dependent on hormones?

Cindy Weeds, the coordinator of women's programming at Planned Parenthood Toronto, explains that North American women have normalized the consumption of hormonal birth control. "Often we see women who come in and all they know about is the pill," she says. Whether this is the cause or the effect of the current contraceptive landscape is difficult to say. Proliferation of hormonal methods is cyclical: As these contraceptives become more accepted, the industry becomes more profitable and advertising increases. This ensures the products stay on the radar and gain approval, relaunching the cycle. "Certain kinds of pills are really heavily marketed, particularly to young women," says Weeds.

One of the consequences of this consumption cycle is a decrease in demand for non-hormonal products, reducing their supply and leading to a dearth of available information.

Other Considerations

Fear of pregnancy is also a consideration. The pill boasts a 99.9 per cent rate of effectiveness, while the diaphragm has a failure rate between four and eight per cent, a margin of error too risky for many.

In Canada, advancements in the study of contraception are not a priority: Little research is done to develop any new methods of birth control, let alone non-hormonal alternatives. Since 2008, the Canadian Institutes of Health Research has spent $916,226 on birth control–related research, none devoted to new developments. In contrast, research devoted to pregnancy and conception received more than $20 million in funding, 22 times the amount allocated to birth control. And for example, while $14,000 was given to a British Columbia conference focused on sexual health education, $20,000 was allocated to finance events honouring the oral contraceptive's 50th anniversary.

Birth control has been lauded as a bastion of feminist liberation and empowerment, but our dependence on hormonal methods is worrisome.

Women will often accept the side effects of hormonal birth control because their fear of conceiving is so great. But, as Amy Sedgwick, owner of Toronto sex and health store the Red Tent Sisters, says, "there's really no other comparable situation where millions of healthy people are taking a daily drug."

Side Effects of Hormonal Contraception

Numerous studies warn of the effects of hormonal contraception. The pill is said to impair muscle gain and increase women's risk of heart attack, stroke and cervical cancer. Studies have also shown that women who use hormonal contraception are more susceptible to mood disorders and sexual dysfunction, and prolonged use of Depo-Provera, the hormonal injection, has been linked to bone density loss.

Birth control has been lauded as a bastion of feminist liberation and empowerment, but our dependence on hormonal methods is worrisome. As women wait longer than ever to have children, they are relying on these drugs and devices for increasing periods of time, sometimes decades. Considering the volume of research revealing frightening long-term effects, hormonal birth control should be dispensed with a plan and a well-thought-out exit strategy. Most importantly, non-hormonal alternatives should be discussed, and used, in Canada.

Hormonal birth control disconnected me from my body and made me feel uncertain about my well-being. Using the FemCap has kept my health and sanity intact, and disturbing instructional video aside, my partner is a big fan. Just don't make him watch it again.

Senegal Needs a Strong International Effort to Fund and Implement Birth Control Programs

Sarah Boseley

Sarah Boseley is a reporter for the Mail & Guardian. *In the following viewpoint, Boseley reports that birth control and family planning programs have been difficult to implement in Senegal for a number of reasons. One is that access to contraception has been limited in many areas, and awareness of birth control and family planning options is scarce. Another has been the interference of the United States, which under the George W. Bush administration funded HIV/AIDS treatment at the expense of birth control programs. This was because the administration was more comfortable treating the disease and not discussing sexual behavior and contraception. Authorities in the region argue that international groups need to be more aggressive in prioritizing access to and education about contraception and family planning in Senegal.*

As you read, consider the following questions:

1. According to Boseley, what percentage of pregnancies in the developing world are unintended?

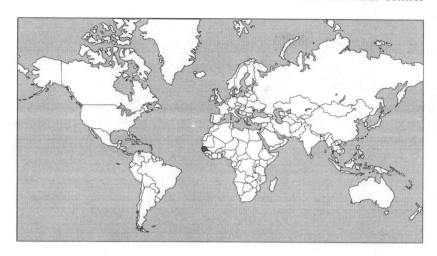

2. How much money does Boseley report that the Gates Foundation is contributing to birth control efforts in developing countries such as Senegal?

3. How much money does the author report the George W. Bush administration pledged to fight AIDS over five years in Africa?

At the back of a clinic in the densely populated Guédi-awaye area, where a tide of rural incomers washes up the edge of urban Dakar, a woman sits waiting with the undemanding endurance of poverty and old age. Nene Ba looks in her 60s. The small child on her lap could be her grandson. But she is 44 and the one-year-old boy is the youngest of her 10 children.

"I am so tired," she says, adding that she had not wanted all these babies. "I didn't know how to stop." Now she does. At the family planning clinic, where she is waiting, her tubes were tied, freeing her of the curse of endless childbearing.

The "Wild West" of Family Planning

Just 20 minutes away at a conference centre in downtown Dakar, the world's largest-ever gathering of exports, advocates and campaigners in birth control is under way. Senegal was chosen because this is what one conference participant called "the Wild Wild West of family planning".

Sub-Saharan Africa teems with small, skinny, ragged children—43% of the population is under 15—but in the Francophone west just 10% of women have access to the hormonal birth control methods that, since the 1960s, have enabled women elsewhere to take control of their fertility and live the life they chose. About 40% of pregnancies in the developing world are unintended and nearly half of those end in mostly unsafe abortion.

In the year when the planet welcomed its seven billionth baby, some may see this as a scandal. When the prime development goal of the moment is cutting maternal mortality, it seems inexplicable.

The Gates Foundation

At the Dakar conference there is evidence that things have begun to shift. The [Bill and Melinda] Gates Foundation is putting in 70 million a year and the United Kingdom, the Netherlands and France are all putting new money into birth control measures.

Improving Life in Senegal

But the need for birth control still outstrips the resources. In Pikine, another district on the outskirts of Dakar, children throng the dusty streets. Sewage and sanitation are bad and some of the concrete houses are flooded regularly.

Forty-six-year-old Fatou Sann is the only person working in a house of 26 people. She sells fish she gets from the central Dakar market. A four-day-old baby is brought out and another of maybe six months sits on someone's lap. Sann has six children herself, which, she says with a robust laugh, is "definitely enough", but these are the babies of sisters-in-law.

The local mayor, Aliou Diouck, talks of families where eight children sleep on the floor. "Here we are in a very poor

The President's Emergency Plan for AIDS Relief (PEPFAR)

Launched in 2003 by President George W. Bush with strong bipartisan support, the U.S. President's Emergency Plan for AIDS Relief (PEPFAR) is America's commitment to fighting the global HIV/AIDS pandemic. Through shared responsibility and smart investments, PEPFAR is saving lives, building more secure families and helping to stabilize fragile nations. With the generous support of the American people, the U.S. government has committed approximately $46 billion to bilateral HIV/AIDS programs, the Global Fund to Fight HIV/AIDS, Tuberculosis and Malaria, and bilateral TB [tuberculosis] programs through fiscal year (FY) 2010.

PEPFAR's success is measured in lives improved and saved. At the midpoint of 2011, PEPFAR directly supported lifesaving antiretroviral treatment for more than 4.5 million men, women and children worldwide—a 160% increase since 2008. In FY 2011, PEPFAR directly supported antiretroviral prophylaxis to prevent HIV infection from mother to child for more than 660,000 pregnant women who tested positive for HIV—a 72% increase since 2008. As a result, 200,000 infants were born HIV free.

Through its bilateral and regional partnerships in over 70 countries, PEPFAR directly supported 13 million people with care and support, including nearly 4.1 million orphans and vulnerable children, in fiscal year 2011 alone. PEPFAR is leading with science and making smart investments to save lives. With continued support from the U.S. Congress, PEPFAR will continue working to meet President [Barack] Obama's goal of treating 6 million people by the end of 2013.

"Funding and Results," US Department of State, 2012.

environment. Men and women do not work. What's going to happen? They will just have sex. When you have nothing to do, it's the main occupation." His own father had several wives and 21 children. Diouck has four of his own and says he and his wife have decided to have no more. He hopes to set an example.

Keeping Contraception Available

But at the health centre in Pikine they say that only 5% to 6% of local women come for family planning. And last year [2010] they had hormonal contraceptives for 80% of the time.

One of the reasons, says Monica Kerrigan, head of family planning at the Gates Foundation, was that orders for supplies went in on the basis of past consumption—which dropped off when stocks ran out. "We have to learn a lot from the HIV world. They made ARVs [antiretroviral drugs to keep HIV in check] a top priority."

HIV/AIDS Funding

HIV comes up a lot when you ask why family planning seems to have made so little progress. American president George [W.] Bush in his 2003 State of the Union address announced a colossal $15 billion to fight AIDS over five years.

Unease about sex, religious beliefs in the United States and elsewhere, women's low status and cultural issues in poor countries have all made family planning a difficult issue to push forward.

Most of the money was for drug treatment, which, says Professor Duff Gillespie of the Bloomberg School of Public Health at Johns Hopkins University, "allowed evangelicals and George Bush to start making large announcements because they were no longer dealing with sexual behaviour. Why was so much money put into HIV treatment but not prevention? What happened [with treatment] is that it took sex out of AIDS."

But Gillespie says that the stagnation of family planning was not solely because of HIV campaigns. The real stagnation came after the Cairo population conference in 1994. That meeting put family planning into a framework of reproductive health rights that focused on sexually transmitted diseases, the empowerment of girls and maternal health issues.

Women's groups were delighted but birth control slipped down the agenda.

Promoting Contraception and Family Planning

Unease about sex, religious beliefs in the United States and elsewhere, women's low status and cultural issues in poor countries have all made family planning a difficult issue to push forward.

Dan Pellegrom, who has been president of the family planning charity Pathfinder International for 26 years, says the movement can be too passive. "I do think we need to push the envelope. In recent years we as a movement have said let's hang on to what we have achieved. That is an argument for retaining the status quo. You don't mobilise people by retaining the status quo."

He would like to see the fight over abortion taken on—the most contentious area of them all, but more family planning means fewer terminations and fewer deaths from backstreet abortions. And it would expose some agendas.

"It is so important for Americans to understand that most of the people who claim to be opposed to abortion are equally opposed to family planning."

Periodical and Internet Sources Bibliography

The following articles have been selected to supplement the diverse views presented in this chapter.

Kasim Saleh Alazzawi
"The Invisible Monster Behind the Arab Spring," *Al Arabiya*, October 21, 2012. http://www.alarabiya.net/views/2012/10/21/245067.html.

Erin Anderssen
"Giving 222 Million Women the Right to Plan Their Families," *Globe & Mail*, July 13, 2012.

Economist
"The One-Child Policy: The Brutal Truth," June 23, 2012.

Belinda Goldsmith
"Arab Spring to Take Years to Improve Women's Rights: Activists," Reuters, December 4, 2012. http://www.reuters.com/article/2012/12/04/us-women-arabspring-idUSBRE8B314F20121204.

Anne Gonschorek
"China's One-Child Policy Conundrum," Al Jazeera, November 15, 2012. http://www.aljazeera.com/indepth/features/2012/11/2012111484022736469.html.

Jerusalem Post
"Ethiopian Birth Control?," December 10, 2012.

Bobby Jindal
"The End of Birth Control Politics," *Wall Street Journal*, December 13, 2012.

Anne Look
"Nigerian President's Call for Birth Control Sparks Debate," Voice of America, June 28, 2012. http://www.voanews.com/content/nigeria-birth-control-debate/1275536.html.

Talila Nesher
"Why Is the Birth Rate in Israel's Ethiopian Community Declining?," *Haaretz*, December 9, 2012.

Chrys Nnabuife
"Nigeria's Overpopulation and Birth Control," *Guardian*, July 15, 2012.

CHAPTER 3

Social and Religious Factors Affecting Access to Birth Control

A Campaign in India to Promote Birth Control Among Muslim Men Draws Controversy

Raul Irani

Raul Irani is a contributor to Open *magazine. In the following viewpoint, he discusses the successful efforts of Dr. Ilias Ali, who has launched a controversial family planning campaign across India. Dr. Ali specializes in no-scalpel vasectomies (NSVs), a reversible procedure that sterilizes men. To counter religious misconceptions about family planning, Dr. Ali cites the Quran and its support of family planning methods, and he has received support from many Muslim leaders. According to Irani, Dr. Ali's efforts have been productive and successful, and he has gained acceptance in India's Muslim communities.*

As you read, consider the following questions:

1. According to the author, when did Dr. Li Shunqiang invent the no-scalpel vasectomy procedure?
2. What does Irani report the fertility rate in India is?
3. How many no-scalpel vasectomies have Dr. Ali and his team performed since 2008, according to the author?

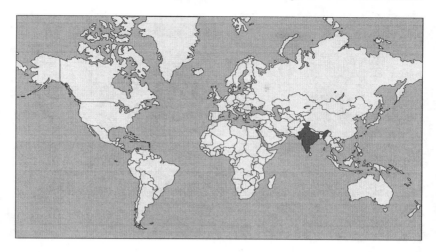

Doctor Ilias Ali is a pious Muslim. But it is not for prayers that he visits different mosques, not only in his hometown Guwahati, but in far-flung areas across Assam. Dr Ali is a sterilisation *jihadi*. Trained in a special vasectomy technique known as 'no-scalpel vasectomy' (NSV), Dr Ali visits mosques to persuade people of his community to keep their family small. Among Assam's indigenous Muslims, whose birthrate is more or less the same as that of Hindus and other communities, it's a message he need not convey. The problem, in his view, is with nonindigenous Muslims, mostly those who have come from East Pakistan (now Bangladesh). Their literacy levels are very low and they hold such superstitious beliefs as children being a blessing from Allah that man has no control over.

To encourage family planning, Dr Ali cites the Quran (Chapter 46, Verse 15): '*Wa hamluhu wa fisaluhu salasuna sahran*' (There should be a gap of 30 months between a child's birth and his/her weaning). Since lactation is understood to act as a natural contraceptive for a mother, this implies that there should be a gap of two-and-a-half years between two children.

The No-Scalpel Vasectomy

The no-scalpel vasectomy is a technique used to do the vasectomy through one single puncture. The puncture is made in the scrotum and requires no suturing or stitches.

The primary difference compared to the conventional vasectomy is that the vas deferens is controlled and grasped by the surgeon in a less traumatic manner. This results in less pain and fewer postoperative complications.

"About the Procedure," NoScalpelVasectomy.com, 2010.
www.noscalpelvasectomy.com.

No-Scalpel Vasectomy

Dr Ali, a surgeon, is currently a professor of surgery and head of the Department of Emergency Medicine at Gauhati Medical College. He underwent NSV training in China under a Chinese surgeon, Dr Li Shunqiang, who invented this procedure in the mid-70s. But it was only in the mid-90s that this simple and hassle-free technique was introduced in India. In this medical procedure for men, the sperm-carrying tubes are blocked by a special instrument through a tiny insertion hole made in each scrotum. No stitches are needed. The best part about it is that it is reversible. It was under Dr Ali's guidance that Assam's first NSV camp was organised in 2008.

A Dangerous Campaign

Dr Ali's campaign has been fraught with danger. Sterilisation is a sensitive issue among Muslims, not just for religious reasons—it's labelled by many as un-Islamic—but also because of a legacy of the Emergency [a period of political unrest in the 1970s], when an enforcement of the procedure on the poor was seen by an appalled minority as a denial of their fundamental reproductive rights.

In 2009, Muslim clerics issued a *fatwa* against Dr Ali, an 'opinion' that can hold considerable weight for believers. His meetings were boycotted and his family members were threatened. His friends and colleagues would fear for his life every time he undertook a long and lonely journey to reach an interior region of Assam to spread his message.

To counter the hostility, Dr Ali began appealing to religious leaders. He put forth examples of countries like Iran and Indonesia. In Iran, family planning was advocated by the Islamic revolutionary Ayatollah Khomeini himself. He made it clear in his speeches that Islam has nothing against limiting the size of one's family. Dr Ali says that over 1993–2004, about 400,000 people underwent NSV in Iran. Today, its fertility rate is 1.88, compared to India's 2.6. In Indonesia, another Muslim country, it is 2.2.

Sterilisation is a sensitive issue among Muslims, not just for religious reasons . . . but also because of a legacy of the Emergency, when an enforcement of the procedure on the poor was seen . . . as a denial of their fundamental reproductive rights.

Polygamy

The doctor also dissuades Muslim men from multiple wives, a practice common among immigrants from East Bengal. To support this, Dr Ali cites the Quran again (Chapter 4, Al Nisaa): 'Faa-in khiftum alla ta'-dilu fawahidatun' (If you fear you will not be able to be equally just with them, then [marry] only one). And then, this: 'Wa lun tasta teeoo un ta'dilue biinal nisaee walaw harastum' (You are never able to be fair and just between women, even if it is your ardent desire). Dr Ali says countries like Turkey and Tunisia have banned polygamy, and that it is subject to administrative or judicial control in Egypt, Syria and Jordan.

After much effort, the doctor's views are gaining acceptance among Assam's Muslim masses, and he has even been invited to religious congregations on some occasions. Barring certain pockets, he says he faces no further resistance to his work now. Since 2008, he and his team have conducted about 36,000 NSVs in addition to 180,000 tubectomies.

Making a Difference

Dr Ali, whose father was a cultivator, had a modest upbringing. Their village had no school. Every morning, he would walk to a neighbouring village to attend a primary school there, one that had no desk nor bench. It was after much hardship that he completed his MBBS [bachelor of medicine and bachelor of surgery] degree. In 1987, he finally got his master's in general surgery. He had married his wife Saira only a year earlier. They now have two children—a girl and a boy. In 2004, the couple started a hospital for the poor. His wife looks after its day-to-day functioning.

Today, Dr Ali's work has transcended borders. He receives invitations from countries like Rwanda and the Philippines to promote NSV. But it is India that concerns Dr Ali most. "Even after so many years of independence, we are still fighting for basic amenities," he says, "One major reason is the population explosion in our country. . . . India cannot develop unless we become serious about controlling it. Look at China, it is progressing like anything."

Afghanistan's Push for Birth Control to Control Population Growth Is Supported by Mullahs

Associated Press

The Associated Press is an American news agency. In the following viewpoint, the author examines the recent campaign in Afghanistan to promote contraception as a way to control the fertility rate and decrease the maternal and infant mortality rates across the country. Key to that effort has been the support of Islamic religious leaders, many of whom endorsed the use of contraception and quoted the Quran to urge couples to take more time between babies to improve the long-term health of infants and mothers. The author maintains that the Afghan Ministry of Public Health has collaborated with nongovernmental organizations and international health organizations to dispel cultural and religious misconceptions, educate religious and community leaders on different forms of birth control, and provide birth control to couples who need it.

As you read, consider the following questions:

1. According to UNICEF, what percentage of couples in Afghanistan use some form of birth control?

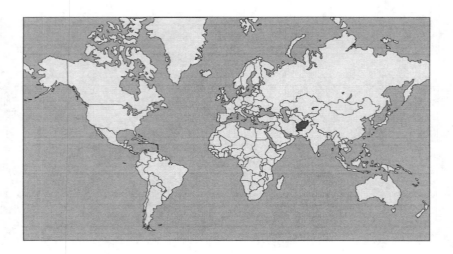

2. What does UNICEF estimate that the maternal death rate is in Afghanistan?

3. How many mullahs does the author report endorsed using contraception as a way to increase the time between births?

Some mullahs in Afghanistan are distributing condoms. Others are quoting the Quran to encourage longer breaks between births. Health experts say contraception is starting to catch on in a country with the world's second highest maternal death rate.

Afghanistan has one of the world's highest fertility rates, averaging more than six babies per woman despite years of war and a severe lack of medical care. Awareness of, and access to, contraceptives remain low among many couples, with UNICEF [the United Nations Children's Fund] estimating 10 percent of women use some form of birth control.

But use of the pill, condoms and injected forms of birth control rose to 27 percent over eight months in three rural areas—up to half the women in one area—once the benefits were explained one-on-one by health workers, according to the report published Monday [March 1, 2010] in *Bulletin*, the World Health Organization's journal.

"The main take-home point is that for women who do not want to be pregnant now, it can be a double tragedy for her to die from a pregnancy she did not want—especially when we could have helped her," said lead author Dr. Douglas Huber, who conducted the study for U.S.-based nonprofit Management Sciences for Health. "The fastest, cheapest, easiest way to reduce maternal deaths in Afghanistan is with contraception."

Afghanistan's maternal death rate of 1,800 per 100,000 live births is topped only by Sierra Leone worldwide, according to UNICEF. The U.S. rate is 11 per 100,000 births.

Islam, unlike Catholicism, does not fundamentally oppose birth control. Everything from vasectomies to abortions [is] supported in various parts of the Muslim world.

Quotes from the Quran

Quotes were used from the Quran to promote breast-feeding for two years, while local religious leaders, or mullahs, joined community and health leaders to explain the importance of spacing out births to give moms and babies the best chance at good health.

In total, 37 mullahs endorsed using contraceptives as a way to increase the time between births, some delivering the message during Friday prayers. The mullahs' major concerns centered on safety and infertility, the report said.

"All the mullahs at the community level knew of these things that the Prophet Muhammad himself advised his followers," Huber said. "This was not a hard sell."

Islam, unlike Catholicism, does not fundamentally oppose birth control. Everything from vasectomies to abortions [is] supported in various parts of the Muslim world.

Many Afghan mullahs are very open about promoting family planning, said Farhad Javid, program director of Marie Stopes International, a British-based family planning organization in Kabul. He was not involved in the study, but said his organization has trained 3,500 religious leaders nationwide on the issue since 2003. It distributed more than 2 million condoms last year.

"In a couple of districts, mullahs were taking our condom stocks and selling them during (night) prayers because the clinics were not open after 4 o'clock," Javid said.

Involving Husbands

During the study from 2005–2006—which involved 3,700 families in three rural areas with different ethnic groups, including both Sunni and Shia Muslims—the [Ministry of Public] Health collaborated with nonprofit organizations to spread the word that using birth control was 300 times safer than giving birth in Afghanistan. They also involved husbands in the project and sought to dispel beliefs that contraceptives have negative side effects, such as infertility.

Dr. Matthews Mathai, a maternal health expert at the World Health Organization in Geneva, cautioned that the program may be difficult to expand nationally due to high costs, intensive training and the country's continuing conflict. He also said some women may prefer to have large families, fearing child deaths.

"It's good to see there are results coming out of Afghanistan," said Mathai, who was not involved in the research. "Clearly, it takes the religious leaders and the men to get some change. It would be good if this could be replicated, but in the long run, it has to be sustainable."

The health ministry plans to expand the program nationally. Huber said USAID [United States Agency for International Development], the European Union and the World

Bank are involved in the scale-up. The pilot study was funded by the William and Flora Hewlett Foundation.

Sexual Health Bill Divides the Philippines

Naomi Conrad

Naomi Conrad is a reporter for Deutsche Welle. In the following viewpoint, she explicates the divisive debate in the Philippines about the sexual and reproductive health bill, which would extend health education in school, improve access to contraception, and enhance prenatal and postnatal care. Conrad reports that the Catholic Church has come out strongly against the bill, arguing that the bill encourages promiscuity and infidelity and will increase the number of illegal abortions. Supporters of the bill contend that it will decrease abortions by making birth control more accessible.

As you read, consider the following questions:

1. According to government figures, the Philippines has the highest rate of what in Southeast Asia?
2. What percentage of Filipinos does Conrad report are Catholic?
3. According to Bishop Gabriel Reyes, to what parts of the birth control bill is he most opposed?

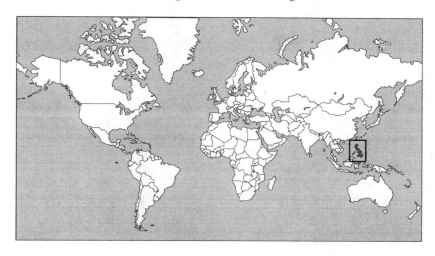

The "love letters" from bishops and priests keep arriving. Raymond Palatino laughed, with just a hint of bitterness. Even primary school kids send him letters, expressing anything but their undying devotion.

"They ask me not to vote for the reproductive health bill," the member of parliament, who is in his early 30s, said before adding that some of the letters can be quite threatening.

Palatino was elected to parliament some three years ago as a member of the Youth Party. Since then, he has been pushing for the sexual and reproductive health bill. . . . The bill was first introduced some 14 years ago, but has been languishing in legal limbo since. It would extend sexual health education in school, make contraceptives more widely available and improve pre and postnatal care. The bill would not legalize abortion.

Choice Between Contraceptives or Food

While contraceptives are legal in the Philippines, they can be expensive and difficult to get. A pack of birth control pills costs between 30 pesos and 50 pesos, just under a euro.

"Often poor families are forced to make a decision: Do I buy one month's supply of contraceptive pills, or do I buy one kilo of rice to feed my family," Amina Evangelista Swanepoel said. She used to work for Human Rights Watch, before starting an NGO that works with women in rural areas.

She is convinced that the bill would greatly improve the lives of the women she works with.

The Catholic Church is heavily involved in politics in the Philippines.

According to government figures, the Philippines has the highest rate of unplanned teenage pregnancies in Southeast Asia. The maternal mortality rate is higher than in neighboring Vietnam. Swanepoel said considering that the Philippines is a democratic state in which women's education is highly valued, which normally correlates with a drop in unplanned pregnancies, "it is really quite shocking how far we still have to go to further sexual and reproductive rights."

Pulpit Preachers Against Contraceptives

The reason why the bill has so far not been passed is because the church hierarchy is strongly opposed to it. "The church is using all its resources and power to prevent the bill," Palatino said.

Emmeline Aglipay agreed. She, too, is a young member of parliament and she, too, has experienced harassment from the church for supporting the bill. When she attends Mass in her local church, the priest singles her out because of her stance of reproductive rights. "It's quite embarrassing for me," she said, her laugh tinged with a degree of bitterness.

Vilifying Defenders

The Catholic Church is heavily involved in politics in the Philippines.

"They do tell parishioners who to vote for," Aglipay said. "Every time someone has lobbied hard for the bill, the Catholic Church will vilify these people in their sermons."

"WHERE'S THE CATHOLIC CHURCH WHEN THEY SPAY OR NEUTER US!"

© Jack Corbett/cartoonstock.com.

The church hierarchy, she added, sends out pastoral letters to churches all over the country, instructing priests to read out the letters during their sermons. Some 80 percent of Filipinos are Catholic and so the church is able to reach many people.

But sometimes, when a priest or bishop rallies against the bill, parishioners will stand up and leave—others demonstrably turn their backs. The majority of Filipinos support the bill, Aglipy said, but the opposition is able to mobilize the media, she said. The last couple of months have seen demonstrations in Manila—both for and against the bill.

"Contraception Encourages Infidelity"

The bill is against the natural moral order, according to Bishop Gabriel Reyes. By promoting contraception, he said, the bill is encouraging promiscuity.

"It also encourages conjugal infidelity," he added. "And history has shown that it reduces the respect for women."

The "good passages of the bill," as Reyes referred to them and which include prenatal care, are already contained in existing legislation, which has yet to be implemented, Reyes said. He added that he is most strongly opposed to the bill's provisions that would make the government responsible for making contraceptives more readily available and promoting sexual education.

Reyes likened these provisions to the government forcing the Philippines' Muslim minority to eat pork.

Divisive Debate

Reyes said he is not against sexual education, but it has to contain values. Otherwise, sexual education will only lead to young people experimenting with sex, leading to higher rates of abortion, he added.

It is the insistence on labeling the bill as an "abortion bill" that frustrates Raymond.

"The bill is really one great measure to prevent abortion, not promote it," he said.

While the Philippines' president Benigno Aquino expressed support for the bill, time is running out.

The bill affirms that abortion is illegal and will remain so. "The issue is so divisive and the debate has become so inflammatory that people are no longer debating the merit of the bill, but rather end up talking about abortion, which isn't even part of the bill," Swanepoel added.

Time Is Running Out

While the Philippines' president Benigno Aquino expressed support for the bill, time is running out. Congress is holding some meetings. But in October, the campaign for the parliamentary election kicks off and those candidates, who are neither strongly in favor of nor opposed to the bill, are unlikely to want to take a stance, Swanepoel said. She added that she is afraid the bill will get sidelined once again, particularly as the current leader of the majority in the Senate and the Senate leader are strongly opposed to the bill and keep on deferring it from the agenda.

"It's mind-boggling that we're still fighting for the very basic right to determine our own body and our own fertility," she said. Meanwhile, Bishop Reyes said he is praying that the bill will not be passed.

Birth Control Access in Guatemala Is Hindered by Religious and Social Pressures

Danilo Valladares

Danilo Valladares is a reporter for Inter Press Service (IPS). In the following viewpoint, he investigates the sharp increase of teen pregnancies in Guatemala, particularly girls as young as ten years old. Valladares reports that authorities blame the lack of sex education in schools and the Catholic Church's opposition to contraception as key factors in the rise. Although Guatemala has renewed family planning efforts—especially in the area of preventing unwanted teen pregnancies—bureaucratic ineptitude has hindered progress. Valladares reports that new legislation has also failed to improve the situation in Guatemala. He concludes that it is essential that deep-seated cultural and religious factors are addressed and overcome in order to make real and lasting progress in controlling the nation's teen pregnancy problem.

As you read, consider the following questions:

1. According to Mirna Montenegro, how many ten-year-old girls in Guatemala had babies in 2011?
2. How many births were there to ten- to fourteen-year-old girls in Guatemala in 2011, according to Montenegro?

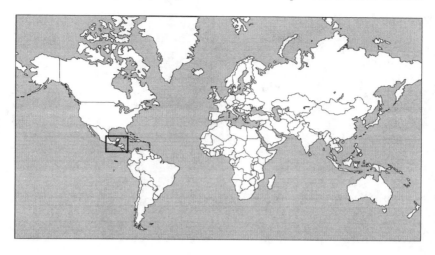

3. According to a 2011 study, what country has the highest adolescent fertility rate in Latin America?

Teenage pregnancies are on the rise in Guatemala, along with the dropout rate in schools, family breakdown and many other related social ills.

A graph of statistics from the Ministry of [Public] Health and Social Assistance shows a rising trend, with 41,529 pregnancies in girls aged 10 to 19 in 2009, 45,048 in 2010 and 49,231 in 2011, giving an average of 135 a day last year [2011].

Contributing Factors

A long list of factors contribute to early motherhood, ranging from lack of sex education to the influence of the Catholic Church's ban on contraceptive use, and impunity for statutory rape, according to Mirna Montenegro of the Sexual and Reproductive Health Observatory, a local NGO [nongovernmental organisation].

"Imagine! In 2011 there were 21 babies born to 10-year-old girls! What's more, we have no social protection system for them," she told IPS [Inter Press Service].

"We are one of the few countries where there are so many pregnancies among 10- to 14-year-old girls. In 2011 alone there were 3,046 births to such young mothers in Guatemala," she said. "Pregnancy in an underage girl is the product of statutory rape, so logically there should be an equal number of court prosecutions under way, but this is not so," she complained.

Montenegro said the Guatemalan justice system finds it problematic to punish offenders in these cases. "The younger the victim, the closer the family ties between herself and the rapist," she said.

The Catholic Church's opposition to using birth control methods and to a comprehensive approach to sexuality that includes avoiding unplanned pregnancy and sexually transmitted diseases is also a hurdle, Montenegro said. "It affects the development of attitudes within the family," she said.

Deep-rooted cultural factors also encourage pregnancies and prevent women from taking advantage of opportunities for a better life.

Launching Family Planning Campaigns

The health and education ministries signed a cooperation agreement in 2010 to implement programmes to prevent unwanted pregnancies in the six provinces with the highest HIV/AIDS incidence, maternal mortality rates and other indicators of concern.

"Progress has been made in raising the awareness of teachers, developing teaching materials and learning modules, and analysing the context of the situation in the provinces. But these things have not yet reached classrooms, as they are bogged down in provincial and ministerial head offices," Montenegro said.

The family planning law, regulations for which were adopted in 2009, brought sex education into primary schools and facilitated access to contraceptive methods. The following year the healthy maternity act was approved, which obliges health authorities to provide basic services and care before, during and after pregnancy.

But the new laws have not been successful in curbing teen pregnancies.

One out of five Guatemalan mothers are aged between 10 and 19, the highest adolescent fertility rate in Latin America, according to a 2011 study on the state of the world's girls, titled "Because I Am a Girl: So, What About Boys?" by Plan International, a child protection agency.

Fighting Cultural Attitudes

Deep-rooted cultural factors also encourage pregnancies and prevent women from taking advantage of opportunities for a better life.

Cecilia Fajardo, a psychologist with the [Association for] Family Welfare of Guatemala (APROFAM), told IPS, "We are still taught that women's role is to be wives and mothers, which is our right, but we are not told about other avenues of self-improvement."

Fajardo said there could be more child and teen pregnancies than those reported by the health ministry, since "many of the births take place at home, or pregnancies are terminated without the authorities' knowledge."

Education Is Key

To help teenagers, APROFAM has created innovative programmes in schools for young people of both sexes to come to grips with practical aspects of pregnancy, fatherhood and motherhood, using aids like the electronic baby and the pregnancy simulator.

"The pregnancy simulator is a strap-on garment with an enlarged bust and belly weighing 25 pounds (11 kilograms), the average weight gain a woman experiences in pregnancy. It enables teenagers to experience 26 different signs and symptoms of pregnancy," Fajardo described.

The electronic baby is a computerised infant-sized doll that mimics the behaviour of a newborn, including crying to signal that it is hungry or tired.

"We give young girls these experiences to give them knowledge about sexuality and reproductive health. We do not impose on them the idea that they should not be mothers," Fajardo said.

This impoverished Central American country of 14 million people has an adolescent (under 20) birthrate of 114 per 1,000 women in rural areas, according to the national mother and child health survey for 2008–2009.

The Consequences of Teen Pregnancy

Silvia Maldonado of the National Alliance of [Organizations for Reproductive Health of] Indigenous Women (ALIANMISAR) told IPS that dropping out of school, malnutrition and discrimination are among the consequences of teen pregnancies.

She said education was one of the most important factors for the prevention of adolescent pregnancy, which severely curtails life opportunities for thousands of teenagers and creates the phenomenon of "kids having kids."

"It is essential to talk about sexuality in schools, and for parents to talk to their children in depth about this issue in order to prevent more teen pregnancies," Maldonado said.

Condoms, Birth Control and Abortion

Independent

The Independent *is a daily newspaper in Uganda. In the following viewpoint, the editorial team assesses the implications of the first national study of induced abortions and postabortion complications in Rwanda. The 2012 study reveals that access to birth control could have prevented most of the unintended pregnancies in the country and would have eliminated the need for many abortions and subsequent complications. Unfortunately, cultural attitudes have discouraged many men and women from obtaining birth control, including condoms. The fact that the study was commissioned and Rwandans are debating its findings, however, may be a sign of an emerging public recognition of the problem and a willingness to find a solution to it.*

As you read, consider the following questions:

1. According to a March 2012 study, how many abortions are performed annually in Rwanda for women aged fifteen to forty-four?

2. What percentage of all pregnancies in Uganda does the same study estimate were unintended in 2009?

3. According to the 2005 Rwanda Demographic and Health Survey, what percentage of women aged fifteen to twenty-four were able to access condoms on their own?

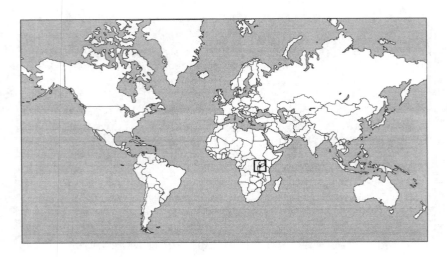

It's a story that repeats itself over and over again in this country: a young girl finds herself pregnant at an untimely moment and is forced to seek an unlawful and dangerous solution to the problem. For Martha (real name held on request), then a high school student in her final year, an abortion was the only avenue to keep open the possibility of pursuing a university degree in human resource management.

"Knowing that I couldn't easily have an abortion here, I desperately went to a neighboring country without my parents' consent because I was going to do this in hiding," she says. "I probably went to a quack medic, and the abortion wasn't done well. In the process, my uterus was damaged after heavy bleeding for days and now I can't have babies anymore."

Abortion has long been an extremely sensitive subject in Rwanda's culturally conservative environment.

The extent of such unfortunate cases was recently documented in a study published in March entitled, "Abortion Incidence and Postabortion Care in Rwanda." The study, the first to provide national- and province-level estimates of induced abortions and postabortion complications, detailed that there are approximately 60,000 abortions annually in Rwanda for women aged 15–44, of which 40% lead to complications.

Accordingly, says the study, one in every five women in Rwanda can expect to "require treatment for complications of an induced abortion over their reproductive lifetimes."

The figures have intensified the debate surrounding abortion in Rwanda and threatens to undermine the country's hopes of achieving the fifth Millennium Development Goal—a 75% reduction in the maternal mortality ratio by 2015—because "the rate of decrease in maternal mortality," says the study, "is much slower than that needed."

Abortion has long been an extremely sensitive subject in Rwanda's culturally conservative environment. According to Jean Claude Rurangwa, a 67-year-old resident of Gasyata, at one time girls who got pregnant outside wedlock could even be thrown over a cliff. Although no such dramatic punishment exists today, women who seek abortions could still be subject to prison sentences of one to five years, while those that facilitate the practice can be sentenced to five to ten years behind bars.

As of now, abortion law, which was put into effect in 1977, maintains that the procedure is permissible to save a woman's life or protect her physical health, so long as the woman can garner the consent of two separate doctors. However, there is ongoing debate in parliament over potential amendments to article 165 of the penal code, amendments that would make it permissible to have an abortion—or assist in an abortion—if the woman is pregnant because of incest, rape, forced marriage or if the pregnancy threatens the health of the unborn baby or the pregnant woman.

But the article, which was approved by the Chamber of Deputies and is now under consideration by the Senate, will not be easy for all of society to swallow, especially the country's respective religious communities.

"Rape shouldn't be a reason for abortion because if you kill the baby and let the rapist live, he will go on raping others, only leading to more abortions," says Most Reverend Emmanuel Kolini from the Anglican Church. "Incest is also unjustifiable since it has always been here, so a child's life shouldn't be terminated simply because the parents are related."

The chairman of Bible Society Rwanda Darius Kankiriho believes there is no justifiable circumstance for an abortion. "No one has the right to decide the fate of the unborn baby," he says. "If their life or that of the mother's is in danger, then let God take the course of action instead of man helping the baby to die."

A delegation of representatives from Christian churches nationwide was recently welcomed by President Kagame to hold a discussion on the subject. The church leaders' influence on social issues, and on Rwandan society as a whole, might explain the abrupt cancellation of a press conference scheduled to publicise the abortion study in March. According to an email from the Health Communication Centre, the cancellation was a result of stakeholders preferring to have a closed-door meeting.

Stern attitudes and abortion laws could also be contributing to the high number of women—a third of the population according to the study—who fail to seek medical assistance, often out of fear, for postabortion complications. This news comes in spite of the fact that 92 percent of all medical facilities in the country treat postabortion complications, and that "public facilities must provide a comprehensive package of services for the management of postabortion complications if they are a referral or district hospital, or a minimum package of services if they are a health center."

According to the director of the Maternal and Child Health Unit at the Ministry of Health Dr. Fidel Ngabo, who helped author the study, medics are meant to offer postabortion treatment to patients regardless of the circumstance and to maintain the privacy of the patients' cases.

However, one way to limit the number of women who show up for such critical assistance, says Chantal Umuhoza, coordinator of Safe Abortion Action Fund (SAAF) project, is to actually legalise the practice. Umuhoza adds that the decision to terminate a pregnancy is an inherent human right— one that should not continue to be violated.

How Did We Get Here?

According to the study, in 2009, 47% of all pregnancies across the country were unintended. Although some resulted from a number of horrible situations such as rape or defilement, the most common cause was a failure to use contraceptives. Birth control is another hotly contested issue in Rwanda because, as the study points out, "social sanctions often prevent [women] from using contraceptives because the practice of contraception among unmarried women is perceived as being an indication of promiscuity."

Unlike in Europe or North America where it is common for girls to discuss their birth control methods with their parents, girls in Rwanda often feel uncomfortable discussing their sexuality with elders. Both sides instead pretend that the young woman is not sexually active, and as a result the need for contraception is not an issue. "My parents would kill me if they knew I was having sex," comments one young woman. "I can't tell them I want to go on birth control!"

But access to birth control, the study points out, does increase the number of safe pregnancies, and in turn, the number of healthy babies. Between 2005 and 2010, after emergency contraception became legal and available in Rwanda, the report points out, the percentage of women in unions using such protection increased from 9% to 44%. During that time, the proportion of births attended by skilled personnel

Abortion Laws

During the nineteenth century, laws restricting abortion were established throughout Europe and the United States. Most governments and Christian churches dropped the concept of ensoulment, deeming the fetus to be life, or potential life, from conception forward. Europeans spread their moral objection to abortion throughout colonies in Africa, Asia, and South America.

By the twentieth century, laws restricting abortion were widespread throughout the world, but legal restrictions did not stop the practice. Abortions were performed in secret at the cost of many women's lives. The high numbers of deaths and severe injuries due to unsafe abortion caused a general rethinking of abortion laws in the second half of the twentieth century in Europe, Asia, and the United States.

By the twenty-first century, abortion was legal for about two-thirds of the world's population, but abortion laws varied widely. In some countries abortion was available on demand (for any reason) throughout some part or all of a pregnancy. In some countries abortion was illegal under all circumstances. Other countries took a middle path. Some of the special circumstances for permitting abortion where it was otherwise illegal included maternal life and health, pregnancy resulting from rape, economic circumstances, and defects in the fetus.

"Abortion," Global Issues in Context Online Collection, 2012.

increased from 39% to 69% and under-five mortality declined from 152 to 76 deaths per 1,000 live births.

In the absence of birth control, condoms provide a dependable alternative, while also protecting the respective partners against STDs and HIV. But even here there has been debate. "People are scared of carrying or possessing condoms," explains Dr. Aflodis Kagaba, the executive director of the Health Development Initiative (HDI), a local nonprofit organization that has toured more than two dozen schools across the country to educate the youth on sexual health and reproductive education (SHARE). "There's a perception that it's immoral to have condoms."

"When we ask young people they say 'we'll have sex when we're married', because that is what their parents have taught them, so it's kept secretive," adds Kagaba. "Because it deviates from the culture, young people are shy to go the pharmacy and pick them up. But if you put the condoms in a bathroom they'll be taken."

HDI has not only worked to educate students about sex but also to increase their accessibility to condoms. According to the 2005 Rwanda Demographic and Health Survey, only 37% of women aged 15–24 reported being able to access condoms on their own, compared with 73% of young men of the same age. It is even more difficult for women in a boarding school, says Kagaba, where condoms are not available and where the need to buy condoms is not a justifiable excuse to leave the school. "Then if a girl has unprotected sex in boarding school, who would she talk to?" he asks. "It's a sin!"

Cultural and religious views opposed to pre-marital sex and abortion is nothing new in Africa.

The Future

As Rwanda continues its ambitious development plan and poverty reduction strategy for 2008–2012—which places a strong emphasis on reproductive health and family planning—and maintains its determination to meet all targets set out in the MDG, there are clearly outstanding issues to address.

Nevertheless, the fact that the country has commissioned and published such a report—the only other published research on this topic to date was a 2004 study of four health districts in Rwanda—shows that there is a desire to at least better comprehend the issue of abortion. Debating amendments to article 165 is another important development.

Moreover, the government's intention to increase access to condoms among women and men aged 15–24 to 60 and 80 percent respectively by this year, and the decision to make the youth the theme of this year's World AIDS Day campaign, shows an acknowledgement that the youth are having sex—whether their parents, teachers and religious leaders want to believe it or not—and as a result all must be done to ensure they practice it safely and responsibly.

Last November, during the 7th annual pediatric conference in Kigali, young Rwandans themselves made an appeal for regular voluntary HIV counseling and testing in schools as a way of increasing awareness. The conference also heard accounts that there is very little information provided to adolescents on how to handle their sexuality. Parents at the conference admitted that in addition to not knowing how to explore the delicate subject with their children, they were worried that even initiating such discussions could lead their children to start experimenting with sex.

Cultural and religious views opposed to pre-marital sex and abortion is nothing new in Africa. In many countries these traditional views continue to inhibit change, while the number of women having abortions across the continent is not declining. Between 2003–2008, according to the Guttmacher Institute—a US-based non-profit organization that seeks to advance sexual and reproductive health through research, policy analysis and public education—the abortion rate in Africa remained at 29 abortions per 1,000 women of childbearing age. Moreover, in 2011, according to the World Health Organization (WHO), unsafe abortion techniques accounted for one in six maternal deaths in East Africa.

These subjects will undoubtedly remain hotly contested and deeply sensitive in this country. Ending a life, even that of a two-week-old fetus, should not be a decision that comes lightly. However, if Rwanda does want to meet its development and health targets, and wants to continue being a role model for its regional neighbors—and for all African countries—such debates between all sides must continue; and the evidence from such laudable reports must be deeply analyzed for the benefit of all Rwandan women.

Japanese Women Do Not Favor the Birth Control Pill

Mariko Kato

Mariko Kato is a staff writer for the Japan Times. *In the following viewpoint, she reports on the slow public acceptance of the birth control pill as a form of contraception in Japan—a situation that some observers call contradictory in light of the country's wide acceptance of abortion as a means of birth control. Kato finds that abortion was legalized in 1948 in Japan, where there are no religious taboos against the practice. When the birth control pill was introduced, however, there was a widespread concern about side effects and its high cost. Some believe that the increasing numbers of Japanese women utilizing the birth control pill will lead to a significant drop in abortions in the coming years.*

As you read, consider the following questions:

1. According to the author, how many abortions have been conducted in Japan every year since the beginning of the twenty-first century?
2. According to a 2008 health ministry study, what percentage of Japanese women take the pill?
3. Why does the author believe that the health ministry finally legalized the birth control pill in Japan in 1999?

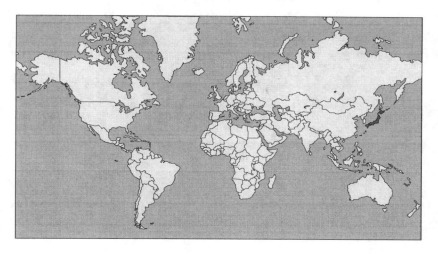

People may be surprised to know abortion has been legal in Japan since 1949, more than a decade earlier than in other industrialized countries.

In subsequent years, abortion became socially accepted to the point that Japan drew international criticism for attracting foreigners seeking to terminate their pregnancies. Since the turn of the 21st century, around 300,000 abortions have been conducted in Japan each year.

Some commentators call Japan's approach to abortion contradictory, comparing it with the belated legalization of the pill, one of the few birth control methods that women can initiate that has a high success rate. This year [2009] marks the 10th anniversary of the introduction of the pill in Japan, and yet the majority of Japanese prefer using condoms, citing the drug's expense and side effects.

So what is the history of abortion and the pill in Japan, and what are the current issues regarding birth control? Here are some questions and answers:

How many abortions are performed in Japan every year?

There were about 256,000 abortions in 2007, or 9.3 per 1,000 women aged 15 to 49, the lowest figure so far, according to the Health, Labour and Welfare Ministry. The number had

been decreasing steadily since the 1950s, when there were between 40 and 50 abortions per 1,000 women of childbearing
age.

---

*This year [2009] marks the 10th anniversary of the in-
troduction of the pill in Japan, and yet the majority of
Japanese prefer using condoms, citing the drug's expense
and side effects.*

One of the main reasons for this trend is the increasing
use of the pill, according to a health ministry report on abortion.

The most oft-cited reason for terminating a pregnancy is
that the couple is not married, accounting for 28 percent of
the 122 women with experience of abortion who were sur-
veyed for the report last year. Financial difficulties came second, with 16 percent.

Roughly 95 percent of abortions in Japan in 2007 took
place in the first 11 weeks of pregnancy, and nearly 8 percent
were conducted on women under age 20.

The 20–24 age bracket had the greatest number of abortions, at 62,500, while 18,600 abortions were performed on
women above 40 years old.

Looking at other industrialized nations, there were 19.4
abortions per 1,000 women aged 15 to 44 in the United States
in 2005, according to the think tank Guttmacher Institute,
while in England and Wales there were 18.2 per 1,000 women
in that age group last year, according to the British government.

*How many women take the pill, and what other contracep-
tives are common?*

Condoms are preferred by nearly 80 percent of married
women in Japan, according to a survey conducted by the
health ministry last year. Only 2.2 percent of women take the

pill, while 16.7 percent prefer their male partner to ejaculate externally and 3.6 percent opt for the rhythm method.

Negligible numbers use other methods common abroad, including the intrauterine device or spermicide.

But use of the pill is on the rise. According to a report by the OC [Oral Contraceptives] Information Center, operated by a group of firms that manufacture the drug, 657,000 women are now using the pill, three times as many as in 2001.

The percentage of Japanese women who take the oral contraceptive is still minimal compared with those in the West, where it is one of the most common forms of birth control.

According to a 2007 report by the U.N. [United Nations] on the types of contraception used by females aged 15 to 49 who are formally or de facto married, 18 percent of those in the U.S. use the pill, while the number is 44 percent in France and 52 percent in Germany.

What historic debates are there regarding abortion in Japan?

Abortion was criminalized in 1880 under the first penal code. Japan had a high birthrate at the time and infanticide was not uncommon.

But after World War II, overpopulation was considered a threat to economic progress in light of the postwar baby boom, and abortion was effectively legalized in 1948 under the Eugenic Protection Law. The government also accepted other contraceptives, including the diaphragm, condoms and spermicide. Previously they were mainly considered ways to prevent sexually transmitted diseases, writes Yasuko Tama in the book *Bosei Ai to iu Seido* (The System Called Maternal Love).

Other reasons for legalization included concerns over back-alley abortions and pressure from doctors who saw abortion as a lucrative source of income.

Under the law, a woman qualified for abortion if she or her partner had a hereditary physical or mental illness or a nonhereditary mental illness. She was also eligible if she had been raped, if childbirth would seriously harm her health, or if she could not afford to raise the child.

The law was revised in 1996 to take out the eugenic component under pressure from advocates for the disabled, and was renamed the Maternal Protection Law.

Abortions may only be performed by a designated doctor who must obtain written consent from the woman and her partner, although in practice the partner's consent is not always available. Usually, only women who are less than 22 weeks pregnant are eligible.

Japan's abortion policy came under fire from other countries in the 1950s and 60s, damaging its reputation at a time when the nation wanted to join the ranks of other developed nations after the war. Whereas abortions were a religious taboo in the West, the practice had no similar constraints here.

"The number of tourists coming to Japan for abortions from other industrialized countries, such as the U.K., the U.S. and France, where abortion was strictly restricted, drew criticism as (Japan had been coined) an abortion paradise," Tama writes.

However, there was some resistance domestically from prolife groups and people who feared that the availability of abortion encouraged irresponsible sex and a deterioration of morals.

What about the pill?

By the time Japan introduced the pill in 1999, it had been the only U.N. member not to approve the contraceptive.

The health ministry was discouraged from legalizing the pill in the 1960s due to pressure from abortion doctors with vested interests, who also expressed concerns over prescription drug abuse and side effects. In 1989, the ministry's pharmaceutical advisory council began deliberating on the drug, but legalization was postponed for a number of reasons, including fear of decline in condom use amid growing numbers of HIV patients.

What Is the Birth Control Pill?

The birth control pill, also known as oral contraceptives or just "the pill," is a medicine taken daily to prevent pregnancy. Some women take the pill for reasons other than preventing pregnancy.

Combined pills contain two hormones, estrogen and progestin. Hormones are chemicals that control how different parts of your body work. These pills are taken every day and prevent pregnancy by keeping the ovaries from releasing eggs. The pills also work by causing the cervical mucus to thicken, which blocks sperm from meeting with and fertilizing an egg.

Progestin-only pills (or "minipills") contain only one hormone, progestin. These pills work mainly by causing the cervical mucus to thicken, which prevents sperm from reaching an egg. Less often, minipills prevent pregnancy by stopping ovaries from releasing eggs.

"Birth Control Pill Fact Sheet,"
US Department of Health and Human Services, 2012.

The government finally legalized the pill in 1999 because of its quick acceptance of the erectile dysfunction drug Viagra earlier that year based on foreign clinical data, observers say. Women's groups and some media reports criticized this as hypocritical, since the government had been debating the health risks of the pill even though it was considered safe abroad.

All contraceptive pills available in Japan are low-dose, according to the clinic of the Japan Family Planning Association, meaning the amount of hormones, and side effects, are kept to minimum levels. The pill is prescribed by an obstetrician, and costs around ¥3,000 a month.

It is not covered by health insurance, and there are extra expenses for initial health tests and regular checkups.

Why were individuals in Japan unenthusiastic about the pill?

The reason lies partly in the availability of abortion, writes Ayako Matsumoto in her book, *Piru wa naze Kangei sarenainoka* (Why the Pill Is Not Welcomed).

Observers say the number of abortions among young people could be reduced if information on the pill became more widespread.

When the pill became available in many parts of the West in the 1960s, abortion was still illegal there, so the pill symbolized the liberation of women as it was a reliable form of contraception that they could control. In comparison, the drug drew criticism in Japan from women themselves who said it burdens them with physical and emotional stress while men escape the responsibility of using contraception, Matsumoto said.

Some also insisted the pill could not be compared with Viagra, saying that medicine like Viagra is used to cure a disorder, whereas the pill distorts the natural patterns of a healthy body.

What are some of the current issues surrounding abortion and the pill?

Observers say the number of abortions among young people could be reduced if information on the pill became more widespread.

There is also concern that the drug's side effects are often misunderstood and exaggerated, and that the expense and regular examinations discourage women.

Even among those who take the pill, 60 percent are worried about side effects and 18 percent are concerned about the cost, according to the OC Information Center.

Periodical and Internet Sources Bibliography

The following articles have been selected to supplement the diverse views presented in this chapter.

Daily Trust	"Row Over Jonathan's Birth Control Plan," June 28, 2012.
Jerome M. Epstein	"Bias Towards Ethiopian Jews," *Jerusalem Post*, December 12, 2012.
Andrew Green	"No Contraceptives Means More Illegal Abortions in Uganda," IPS, November 14, 2012. http://www.ipsnews.net/2012/11/no-contraceptives-means-more-illegal-abortions-in-uganda.
Aunohita Mojumdar	"Family Planning: One Afghan Woman's Struggle to Access Contraception," *Guardian*, July 11, 2012.
Cahir O'Doherty	"Why the Catholic Church Is Wrong, Yet Again, with Contraception Lawsuit," *IrishCentral*, May 23, 2012. http://www.irishcentral.com/story/ent/manhattan_diary/why-the-catholic-church-is-wrong-yet-again-with-contraception-law-suit-153054825.html.
Kristin Palitza	"Men Still Make the Decisions on Reproductive Rights in Côte d'Ivoire," IPS, March 15, 2012. http://www.ipsnews.net/2012/03/men-still-make-the-decisions-on-reproductive-rights-in-cote-drsquoivoire.
John Stoehr	"Campaign Against Birth Control Is Religious Fanaticism," Al Jazeera, February 20, 2012. http://www.aljazeera.com/indepth/opinion/2012/02/2012218153227222426.html.
Kenneth R. Weiss	"Philippines Birth Control: Filipinos Want It, Priests Don't," *Los Angeles Times*, July 22, 2012.
Sevira Wirawan	"The Debate over Sex Education," *Jakarta Post*, July 26, 2012.

CHAPTER 4

The Economics of Birth Control Access

Many Slovak Women Find the Cost of Birth Control Prohibitive

Center for Reproductive Rights

The Center for Reproductive Rights is a global legal advocacy organization. In the following viewpoint, the center discusses the findings of a new report that shows that many Slovak women cannot afford the high cost of contraception. To make the situation worse, the Slovak Ministry of Health will not be including contraceptive coverage in its public health insurance package. The center argues that this is a clear violation of international human rights law, which requires states to provide access to a full range of affordable health services. To prevent unwanted pregnancy in Slovakia, the author maintains, the government should be guaranteeing access to affordable contraceptives and working to include contraceptive coverage in any health insurance package. This will satisfy international human rights law and bring Slovakia in line with other European Union (EU) countries.

As you read, consider the following questions:

1. According to the author, in what year did the Parliamentary Assembly of the Council of Europe (PACE) adopt a resolution to urge states to make contraceptives accessible and affordable?

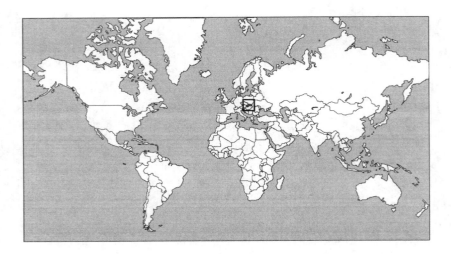

2. How many Slovak women of reproductive age used hormonal contraception in 2008, according to estimates?

3. How many of the twenty-seven European Union (EU) states include contraceptives in their public health insurance packages?

Women and adolescent girls in Slovakia face numerous barriers to accessing modern contraceptives and contraceptive information. Because contraceptives are not covered by public health insurance, their users must pay the full price out of pocket. Some women and adolescent girls—especially the most vulnerable ones, such as those with low incomes or in violent relationships—lack the means to do so. Others are forced by the high cost of hormonal contraceptives to resort to low-quality versions that may not be best suited for them or to unreliable traditional methods of family planning such as coitus interruptus (withdrawal). One month's supply of oral contraception ranges from 7 euros (€) to over €15; a one-time dose of emergency contraception costs about €22; and an intrauterine device costs about €158—prices that are out of reach for many women. The latest available figures, from 2009, put the median monthly income for women in

Slovakia at €562.51. The poverty line for a one-person household was €283 per month, and up to 11.9% of women were at risk of poverty in 2009. For young women, the costs are also prohibitive. As one pharmacist noted, young women often cannot afford emergency contraception and instead opt to purchase a pregnancy test at less than one-fifth the cost.

The lack of accurate, unbiased, and comprehensive information on family planning methods further inhibits women's and adolescent girls' access to modern contraceptives. In many schools, sexuality education is either lacking altogether or inadequate, focusing only on reproductive organs and influenced by the religious views of teachers or administrators. The Catholic Church hierarchy, which plays an important role in Slovak politics and communities, actively advocates against the use of modern contraceptives and promotes traditional methods of family planning, such as periodic abstinence, which are often ineffective. Gynecologists frequently lack the time or will to appropriately discuss contraceptives with their patients. As a result, misinformation and myths about the side effects of contraceptives abound, undermining their use. It is not surprising, then, that use of hormonal contraceptives remains low, at 22.3%, while use of withdrawal as a family planning method is at approximately 32%. These figures stand in stark contrast to those of other European Union [EU] countries, the majority of which subsidize contraceptives through public health insurance. In France, for example, 43.8% of women use the pill and only 3.1% rely on withdrawal; and in Germany, over 50% use the pill and only 0.5% rely on withdrawal.

The Slovak government's failure to address the multiple barriers that women and adolescent girls face in accessing contraception runs counter to its obligations under national, regional, and international law, and defies sound public policy considerations. At the national level, the Slovak constitution guarantees the rights to health, to information, and to nondiscrimination on the basis of sex. Domestic legislation further explicitly mandates the government to provide women with access to prescription contraceptives free of charge. However, these provisions are ignored.

Slovakia is also party to numerous regional and international human rights instruments that require states to ensure that women and adolescent girls have access to a full range of sexual and reproductive health services. This obligation entails making acceptable and affordable contraceptive methods available, as well as making accurate information on those methods available—including by requiring sexuality education in schools. At the regional level, the European Committee of Social Rights, for example, requires member states to ensure that sexuality education is "provided throughout the entire period of schooling," "forms part of the ordinary school curriculum," that such education is "adequate in quantitative terms," and that it is "objective, based on contemporary scientific evidence and does not involve censoring, withholding or intentionally misrepresenting information, for example as regards contraception and different means of maintaining sexual and reproductive health." At the international level, binding human rights treaties such as the Convention on the Elimination of All Forms of Discrimination Against Women require states to eliminate discrimination against women in all spheres of life, including access to health care.

In 2008, the committee that monitors the convention emphasized that family planning services in Slovakia, of which contraceptives form an integral part, fell short of what is required under international law. The committee urged the government "to take measures to increase the access of women and adolescent girls to affordable . . . reproductive healthcare, and to increase access to information and affordable means of family planning. . . ." Slovakia is thus aware that human rights violations are occurring. Furthermore, the government may not use its own failure to collect adequate data on indicators such as the unmet need for family planning—which it is required to do under international law and which would enable it to develop effective policies—as a way to escape accountability.

Ensuring women's access to acceptable and affordable contraceptives is not only required by law but also sound policy from an economic and public health perspective. An increase in contraceptive use reduces the number of unintended pregnancies, which, in turn, leads to savings in health care costs. Moreover, fewer unintended pregnancies benefit women's health by lowering the number of induced abortions and reducing maternal morbidity and mortality. The World Health Organization recognized the health and cost benefits when it included contraceptives, including emergency contraception, in its list of essential drugs that states should make affordable to all. Also aware of these benefits, 18 of 27 European Union member states agreed to fully or partially cover the cost of contraceptives through their public health insurance schemes. Yet, in Slovakia, with the exception of sterilization on health grounds, contraceptives for pregnancy prevention fall completely outside the scope of public health insurance. . . .

Governments have clear international human rights obligations—as well as compelling economic, social, and public health reasons—to ensure women's access to affordable and acceptable contraceptives.

The Right to Contraceptive Services and Information

International human rights law requires states to provide women with access to a full range of sexual and reproductive health services, which includes making acceptable and affordable contraceptive methods available. It also includes providing sufficient and appropriate information on those methods. These obligations are grounded in numerous internationally recognized human rights, including the rights to equality and nondiscrimination, the right to privacy, the right to decide the number and spacing of children, and the right to health.

The ESCR [Economic Social and Cultural Rights] Committee has made clear that the right to health encompasses the right to sexual and reproductive health, which obligates states to ensure affordable access to contraceptives and family planning information. The committee has explicitly stated that all drugs on the World Health Organization (WHO) Model List of Essential Medicines, which includes contraceptives and emergency contraception, should be made accessible to all. It has also expressed the view that lack of access to contraception and to sexuality education are violations of the right to health. States thus have an obligation to provide all women with access to affordable, acceptable, and good-quality contraceptives. At the regional level, the Parliamentary Assembly of the Council of Europe (PACE)—the representative body of Europe's human rights system, the Council of Europe—adopted a resolution in 2008 urging states to make contraceptives accessible and affordable, as well as ensure sexuality education in schools in order to prevent unwanted pregnancies and avoidable abortions. Moreover, denying access to services that only women need violates their fundamental rights to equality and nondiscrimination—hallmark principles of international human rights law enshrined in major regional and international treaties.

Regional and international human rights standards pay special attention to marginalized women—for example, poor women, women in rural areas, and young women—regarding information on and access to contraceptives. In addition, to ensure that states are fulfilling their human rights obligations, regional and international legal instruments underscore the importance of data collection on women's status, health indicators, and education, disaggregated by relevant grounds, including gender, age, and ethnicity.

Governments have clear international human rights obligations—as well as compelling economic, social, and public health reasons—to ensure women's access to affordable and acceptable contraceptives and information and to collect data on the realization of those obligations. However, the Slovak government has largely ignored these obligations and policy justifications. The Committee on the Elimination of Discrimination Against Women (CEDAW Committee) recognized this failure in 2008 when it emphasized that family planning services in Slovakia, of which contraceptives form an integral part, fell short of what is required under international law. The committee urged the government "to take measures to increase the access of women and adolescent girls to affordable ... reproductive health care, and to increase access to information and affordable means of family planning. . . ." The findings of this report bolster the CEDAW Committee's observations and reveal that women in Slovakia face significant barriers to accessing contraceptives. . . .

Lack of Contraceptive Coverage

With the exception of emergency contraception, which is available over the counter, female hormonal contraception can be obtained only by prescription from a gynecologist, whom women may visit without a referral from a primary care physician. Such contraception includes pills, patches, injectables, vaginal rings, and implants. Slovakia's public health insurance scheme, which is mandatory for the entire population, does not cover hormonal contraceptives, thus requiring women to pay for these items out of pocket. This policy exists despite the fact that Slovakia's abortion law seeks to prevent unintended pregnancy by requiring that prescription contraceptives "be provided to a woman free of charge." Furthermore, Slovakia's requirements for including a drug on the list of medicinal products covered by public health insurance include the drug's lifesaving, curative, or preventative qualities. The

Lack of Information and Sexuality Education in Slovakia

Women and adolescent girls in Slovakia not only lack access to contraceptives covered by public health insurance but also suffer from serious barriers to information on contraceptives, which may contribute to the country's low usage rates. Knowledge of modern prevention methods is generally poor; doctors seldom counsel patients sufficiently on the subject; sexuality education in schools is frequently inadequate or absent; and the Catholic Church hierarchy consistently tries to impose its traditional and often discriminatory views on politicians and the public.

In addition, in February 2010, Catholic conservative parliamentarians introduced a bill that would require health professionals to wrongly inform patients that hormonal contraceptives are abortifacients. The bill also proposed to place this inaccurate information on contraceptive packaging. It further included an informed-consent provision that imposed a duty on health professionals to provide women with information on the "potential physical and psychological risks" of hormonal contraception and on resources about alternatives to hormonal contraception provided by civil society groups and religious associations. While the bill did not pass, the number of parliamentarians who voted in favor of it or abstained is alarming and points to, among other things, a lack of knowledge of sexual and reproductive health issues and growing opposition to reproductive rights issues among elected representatives across the political spectrum.

"Calculated Injustice: The Slovak Republic's Failure to Ensure Access to Contraceptives," Center for Reproductive Rights, 2011, p. 24.

only insured contraceptive method is surgical sterilization, which is permanent and irreversible and covered only when there are health indications. Therefore, women to whom pregnancy poses a health risk are given no other option under health insurance besides sterilization. The state also does not subsidize emergency contraception in any way.

Slovakia is not the only EU [European Union] country in which the high price of contraceptives is a barrier to access.

Low Contraceptive Use and Gaps Between European Union Countries

Contraceptive use in Slovakia has improved since the early 1990s, when only 2.2% of women of reproductive age were using hormonal contraception. In 2008, the percentage increased tenfold to 22.3%. Yet, this figure remains low in comparison with other EU countries. In neighboring Czech Republic, 47.4% of women of reproductive age were using hormonal contraception in 2008. In France, 43.8% of women were using the pill in 2009, and use of contraceptive pills in Germany is among the highest in the world, at over 50%.

When comparing overall data from the new European Union (EU) member states of central and eastern Europe (CEE) to that of older EU member states, serious gaps emerge. Prevalence of modern methods (including not just hormonal contraceptives, but also IUDs [intrauterine devices], female sterilization, and male condoms) stands at 36% in some countries of the CEE region—namely, Bulgaria, Czech Republic, Hungary, Poland, Romania, and Slovakia, which are all new EU member states. This is nearly twice as low as in western European countries, where the prevalence is on average 71%. For example, 28% of women in Poland and 40% of women in Bulgaria are using modern contraceptives, compared to 77% and 82% of women in France and the United Kingdom, respectively. This disparity indicates that contraceptive use is an issue worthy of attention across Europe.

Lack of Comprehensive Data on Reproductive Health Indicators

Like many other governments in the CEE region, the Slovak government does not gather comprehensive data on reproductive health indicators, such as unintended pregnancies, contraceptive use, and the unmet need for contraception. The limited data that the state gathers on the prevalence of just a few contraceptive methods—namely, hormonal contraception and IUDs—is insufficient for understanding the reasons behind low usage rates in Slovakia. As a result, it is difficult to effectively identify measures that should be taken to meet the contraceptive needs of women and adolescent girls. Furthermore, public officials are able to remain unaccountable for neglecting to adequately address the health needs of the public due to their own failure to collect adequate and reliable data. . . .

Comparing European Countries' Subsidizations and Their Justifications

Slovakia is not the only EU country in which the high price of contraceptives is a barrier to access; in other new member states, it is a problem as well. To effectively deal with this issue, state subsidization of reproductive health care services in the form of basic public health insurance is widely considered an appropriate measure. Of the twenty-seven EU member states, eighteen include contraceptives in their public health insurance packages as a means to prevent pregnancy without there having to be an underlying health condition. Those states either fully or partially subsidize some hormonal contraceptive methods for all women, for low-income women, or for women under a certain age. However, the remaining nine EU member states do not provide subsidies for hormonal contraceptives, despite their inclusion on the WHO's essential medicines list. All but one of these nine countries are new member states, among them Slovakia. Some of those same countries, including Slovakia, also either do not have national strategies for ensuring access to reproductive health care services or do not have effective strategies for making contraceptives affordable.

EU member states that subsidize contraceptives do so on public health grounds or to uphold fundamental rights. The Slovenian government, for example, considers family planning a fundamental human right guaranteed by the constitution, which grants all citizens the right to determine whether to bear children. In Poland, while the ombudsman for human rights found the withdrawal of subsidies for contraceptives to constitute discrimination on the ground of sex, the government has failed to reinstitute their subsidization. The Belgian Constitutional Court, in addressing the constitutionality of the law on pricing for pharmaceuticals, stated generally that the pricing scheme aims to improve access to drugs that promote public health and social benefits. The court noted that contraceptives are a type of drug that must be accessible to the public at an affordable price. It explained that providing access to them is justifiable on the grounds of public health and social protection in order to reduce the number of unwanted pregnancies. Similarly, the Danish government considers family planning services, including subsidization of contraception, "an integral part of the national health service." In France, research conducted by public authorities on the use of various oral contraceptives indicated that contraceptive subsidies "present an interest in terms of public health." Also espousing the public health argument, the United Kingdom's National Health Service Act mandates that contraceptives be available free of charge to "cut down the number of unwanted pregnancies and . . . decrease the number of abortions." . . .

Unaffordability

When asked whether she offers patients different contraceptive options, Dr. Elena Molnárová, a gynecologist, responded:

> I tell [a woman] about the possibilities and she tells me her financial limit. I tell her what I think is the best and most suitable for her, but the crucial thing is what she can afford. It has happened to me that a patient wanted to take more expensive contraception and she didn't buy it because she couldn't afford it, and she got pregnant. . . .

Beáta, a 40-year-old mother of two, noted that of her approximately 30 female acquaintances, only one is using modern contraception. She explained why this figure is so low:

> I think the main reason is first and foremost financial, that they cannot afford it. Simply in the case of some of my acquaintances or friends it's either that she doesn't work or her husband doesn't work, they have two to three children, it is a problem to [get by], you understand. So I think it is a financial problem. . . .

Ms. Vargová, a pharmacist, has noted that emergency contraception is prohibitively expensive (€22) for young women, particularly students, who lack income. She noted that when some of her customers see the price of emergency contraception, they realize that they cannot afford it and purchase a pregnancy test instead. . . .

Ms. Apolónia Sejková, director of the NGO [nongovernmental organization] MyMamy, which provides support to women subjected to male violence, explained the following:

> Abused women have complained about [their husbands not giving them money for] contraception. It is on the list of things that they do not have buying power after the abuse starts. . . . It is true that abusing men often use conception of more and more children for stronger control and for restricting the partner. In the socioeconomic situation most of

our clients are in, and in general most of the average population of eastern Slovakia, it is difficult to [come up with] any solution. If you have four or five children, no income, live in the house that belongs to the husband or his family, ... [it is] difficult to leave the husband. Many women therefore stay in violent relationships because they take it as at least they have basic living needs covered and they rather stand to be hit or humiliated. . . . They feel that it is the only way for their survival. . . .

Other Structural Barriers

Klaudia, a 36-year-old mother of one, said that daughters of her Catholic friends go to meetings with Salesians, a Roman Catholic religious order, where they also receive information on contraception. However, the information provided is one-sided, focusing on natural family planning and the negative side effects of hormonal contraception.

Speaking about the Catholic Church hierarchy's influence on women's contraceptive use [one woman] observed with apparent sarcasm:

> The church gives [women] a great option: don't use withdrawal, don't use contraception, bring up your child on your own, and don't go for abortion. And that is really great, really great. . . .

According to Ms. Olga Pietruchová, executive director of the Slovak Family Planning Association, access to contraception is impeded by conservative Catholic groups and individuals who spread half-truths and demonize contraception:

> Ideologically-based groups—have a big influence on power, either through the Catholic Church hierarchy or through some political parties. . . . These groups, which include some NGOs and doctors, run negative campaigns, primarily against hormonal contraception by pointing to its negative side effects. But the information [they provide] is partial;

they say one thing but don't say the rest. They always talk about negatives [and] this dominates the public discussion. . . .

According to Dr. Molnárová, the lack of access to contraceptives has to do with the way schools provide sexuality education:

[N]owadays, at many secondary schools there is sexual education, which is taught by catechists, or people who are from different parishes, and [their] explanation of this area is pronouncedly one-sided. . . . We still have a problem [establishing] sexual education within the framework of classes at school. It's still more or less up to biology teachers. In fact, it depends on the professor's view in what direction it all goes.

Ms. Pietruchová of the Slovak Family Planning Association also cited lack of adequate sexuality education as a problem:

Sex education—that is, "Education for Marriage and Parenthood"—is not a mandatory subject, but if the school chooses to teach it, it should do it according to [official school] guidelines [set by the ministry of education]. However, these guidelines are very general; anything can be included under the topics addressed. Moreover, the name of the subject itself—"Education for Marriage and Parenthood"—is sick.

Dutch Legislators Are Debating a New Law Forcing Unfit Mothers to Take Birth Control

Minette Marrin

Minette Marrin is an author, broadcaster, and columnist for the Sunday Times. *In the following viewpoint, she examines a controversial proposed bill before the Dutch parliament that recommends that unfit mothers should be forced by law to take two years of contraception in order to prevent them from having more children. The two-year period is meant to provide the time for the family situation to improve. Marrin acknowledges that although this proposed law is extreme, it is trying to address the very serious problem of unfit mothers having large families. Children born to inadequate mothers are more likely to have significant behavioral problems in school that can lead to unemployment, crime, and drug addiction later in life. She proposes that it might be better for the state to provide incentives for limiting the number of children in such families than to force temporary sterilization.*

As you read, consider the following questions:

1. What Dutch politician is putting forth the controversial bill, according to Marrin?

2. According to Michael Gove, how many children aged five or younger were suspended in Britain because of troubled and violent behavior?

3. What does Marrin view as the problem with taxing unfit parents instead of temporarily sterilizing mothers?

The Dutch are odd. They seem so moderate, so practical, so sensible—a nation of considerate egalitarian cyclists— yet they take their virtues to extremes. They pursue common sense to a fault. For instance, there are plenty of arguments in favour of mercy killing, yet few nations feel quite able to make it legal. The Dutch did, with enthusiasm, long ago. The same is true of legalising cannabis and prostitution.

A Controversial New Bill

Another example of this tendency emerged last week [in November 2008]. Reports hit the blogosphere that a Dutch socialist politician, Marjo Van Dijken of the PvdA party (the social democratic Labour Party), is putting a draft bill before the Dutch parliament recommending that unfit mothers should be forced by law into two years of contraception. Any babies willfully conceived in that period should be confiscated at birth. Unfit mothers would mean those who have already been in serious trouble because of their bad parenting.

There is, I suppose, a grain of common sense behind all that, but Van Dijken has taken it to what seem like scary extremes. One imagines Dutch do-gooders on bikes, descending on all the imperfect mothers of Holland and bearing away their babies in countless bicycle baskets, like totalitarian ex post facto storks.

In person Van Dijken sounds less alarming. She explains that the professionals who come into contact with families in difficulties all say the same thing. They see the same problems repeated again and again in certain families. It's obvious from when social workers are forced to take the first child into care that it won't be the last.

Van Dijken's idea is to try to prevent a new pregnancy in a family whose existing children are already in care until the situation has improved enough for them to be able to come back home. Two years might be a suitable period. If, after the suggested two years of compulsory contraception, the family is still not safe for children, the contraception order could be extended by a judge's review. "If there's a better way, a less invasive way, I will never mention my proposals again," she says.

One imagines Dutch do-gooders on bikes, descending on all the imperfect mothers of Holland and bearing away their babies in countless bicycle baskets, like totalitarian ex post facto storks.

A Serious Problem

If hers is not the answer to the problem, the question remains: What should be done about unfit parents? Children are increasingly being damaged by them. At the extremes, chaotic mothers who are prostitutes or addicts or mentally ill or just what my own mother called inadequate are condemning their children to the same miserable and disordered lives. Man hands on misery to man, as [English poet and novelist] Philip Larkin wrote, and so does woman.

Less extremely, many children are also being damaged by parents who are not so obviously unfit, but still bad enough to do serious harm. On Friday questions by Michael Gove, the shadow education secretary, revealed that more than 4,000 children aged five or under were suspended from school in Britain because of their troubled and violent behaviour. Of the 400 suspensions of children aged just two and three, 310 involved physical assault and threatening behaviour. Numbers of exclusion in all groups under 11 are increasing, mostly because of uncontrolled or violent behaviour.

According to Mick Brookes, general secretary of the National Association of Head Teachers, nursery and primary schools are seeing more parents who have simply lost control: "It's down to poor parenting." Very bad behaviour at school at an early age is just the tip of a disastrous iceberg; hidden under the surface lies a future of illiteracy, unemployment, crime, broken relationships and unhappiness.

Even before children of unfit parents get to schools, their destiny is blighted. Increasingly scientists are beginning to understand that neglect retards cognitive development or impairs it—as with the extreme cases of children in Romanian orphanages, who have never recovered from the personal and sensory deprivation they suffered. Language skills and social skills not learnt in infancy may never be learnt; trauma will be hardwired into the brain.

In plain English, an infant whose mother never reads or plays with him or her, who is constantly uncertain what will happen next and whether he or she will eat, or whether the mother will be enraged or demanding or high, is a child with a permanently damaged future. The cost of bad parents to such an individual is terrible, but it is also very high to the rest of society.

Finding the Moral Way Forward

Given all that, it cannot be right for inadequate mothers to go on giving birth to babies who are destined to be damaged and to inflict damage on others. Equally, it seems wrong to think of interfering with a woman's freedom to have a baby. So we are left with the question of which evil is greater—interference with the mother's freedom or the damage to her child and to society.

As [nineteenth-century British philosopher] John Stuart Mill said: "To bring a child into existence without a fair prospect of being able, not only to provide food for its body, but instruction and training for its mind, is a moral crime, both against the unfortunate offspring and against society." A moral crime, I agree. But Mill goes on to say that "if the parent does

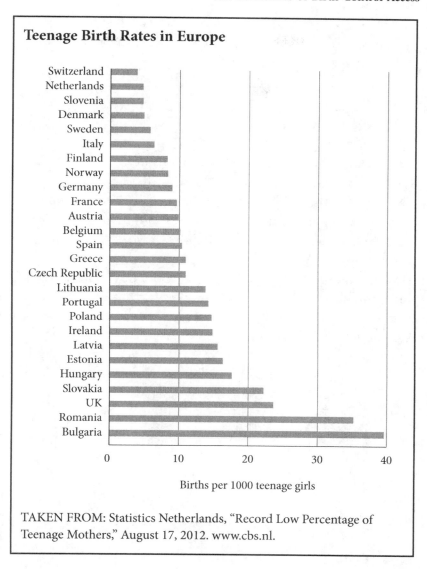

Teenage Birth Rates in Europe

Births per 1000 teenage girls

TAKEN FROM: Statistics Netherlands, "Record Low Percentage of Teenage Mothers," August 17, 2012. www.cbs.nl.

not fulfill this obligation, the state ought to see it fulfilled, at the charge, as far as possible, of the parent".

Taxing unfit parents, rather than temporarily sterilising unfit mothers, might seem more acceptable. But there are several glaring problems with this solution, too. Such parents won't have any money to tax. And besides, the most unfit par-

ent of all is the state; in this country its nurslings are con-
demned to exceptionally high rates of illiteracy, poverty, crime
and mental illness.

---

*Even before children of unfit parents get to schools, their
destiny is blighted.*

On Mill's argument, the state here ought to be taxed for
the disastrous treatment of its "looked-after" children. A sim-
pler way to reduce the number of damaged children would be
to give parents incentives not to have more than two children;
after two, benefits would be withdrawn and larger housing
could be withheld.

It seems to me unfair to deny people any children at all.
But it might be right to reduce the number to two. That would
be fairer to taxpayers than expecting them to support families
larger than their own and it might persuade genuinely unfit
mothers that it is not in their interests to keep producing babies; they will be better off without.

It is time that, like Van Dijken, we started asking these extreme questions.

The Chilean Controversy over Affordable Emergency Contraception Is a Political Issue

Angela Castellanos

Angela Castellanos is a journalist. In the following viewpoint, she traces the struggle over the distribution of emergency contraceptive pills in Chile, where women's rights are hotly contested and the Catholic Church has influence over politics and public opinion. Castellanos reports that the efforts of the Chilean government to provide free emergency contraceptives to all women from fourteen years of age who need it from public health care centers was stymied by the Constitutional Court of Chile, which ruled that such contraceptives are unconstitutional because they are abortifacients, or can cause abortions. This ruling was highly controversial because the strong majority of medical research and opinion does not agree that emergency contraception is an abortifacient. In response, Chilean legislators are working to pass bills that will allow the free distribution of emergency contraceptives in the public health system.

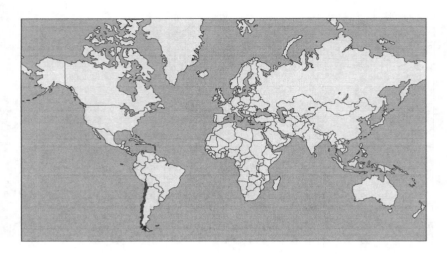

As you read, consider the following questions:

1. According to Castellanos, when did the Constitutional Court of Chile ban free distribution of the emergency contraceptive (EC) pill in the public health system?

2. Which political party does the author identify as having voted against the 2009 bill that found a way to distribute EC for free in the public health system?

3. What kind of EC was authorized for sale in Chilean pharmacies in October 2009, according to Castellanos?

In Chile, women's rights are perhaps even more contested than in other countries in Latin America. It is the only country in the region where the law grants men the right to "manage the patrimony" of their marriage. It was the last country in the region to legalize divorce. And it is one of the few countries in the world where therapeutic abortion is criminalized.

Emergency Contraceptive in Chile

On April 4th 2008, the Constitutional Court of Chile banned free distribution of the emergency contraceptive (EC) pill in the public health system. The judicial ruling came after a debate on the reform of the national norms on fertility regulation (2006), which had resulted in introduction and free distribution of EC by public health care centers to all women from 14 years of age, without their parents' consent. Opponents of birth control objected to the reform, so Chilean president Michelle Bachelet secured access to EC by virtue of an executive order. However, the judicial ruling annulled the reform and Bachelet's order, deciding that the distribution of EC was unconstitutional because, according to the justices, the hormone levonorgestrel, contained in the EC pills, is "abortive", and therefore against the right to life.

In Chile, a high number of illegal abortions and teen pregnancies present serious challenges to a government which has made reducing both abortion and unintended pregnancy a focal point of its reproductive health policy.

As a result of the court decision, EC was partially removed from pharmacies, whereas other pills containing levonorgestrel continued to be sold, but for a price that not all women can afford.

In Chile, a high number of illegal abortions and teen pregnancies present serious challenges to a government which has made reducing both abortion and unintended pregnancy a focal point of its reproductive health policy. So even despite the court ruling on EC, Bachelet's administration continued to seek new legal mechanisms to ensure access for all women—poor and rich alike—to emergency contraception.

The government introduced a bill to regulate information and distribution of contraception methods. Last July [2009] the lower house of the parliament of Chile passed the bill, which allows—among other measures—the free distribution of EC in the public health system.

The bill aimed to guarantee "every person, regardless of their economic situation" free access to the pill.

"The state isn't imposing anything on anyone," Bachelet said. "Each person may decide on her own, but the state must guarantee equal conditions of access to birth control methods."

A vast majority of the legislators voted in favor of the bill—73 votes for, 34 against, and 2 lawmakers abstained from voting. All the votes against the bill were from members of the party Unión Demócrata Independiente, which has linkages with the Opus Dei organization [a conservative Catholic group]. The feminist organizations celebrated the results while the Catholic Church denounced it.

EC and Its Political Implications

Now the bill awaits Senate approval. Meanwhile, Chile is in the midst of an electoral campaign, a circumstance which certainly will have an influence on the votes in the Senate, with presidential candidates on the left and right seeking to assure their potential supporters of their own position on this and other issues. Candidates include Christian Democrat Eduardo Frei, who just three years ago sided with "pro-life" organizations and Catholics against the distribution of the pill. On the other hand is the right-wing candidate Sebastián Piñera, whose coalition also firmly backs the prohibition.

As if the debate was not already hot enough, this October the Ministerio de Salud Pública (Ministry of Health) of Chile authorized the sale of the EC pill "Escapel-1" in pharmacies. Conservative members of parliament reacted against the decision, insisting that Escapel-1 has levonorgestrel, the hormone they declare to be "abortive". The conservative movement "Red por la Vida y la Familia" (Network for Life and Family), through its lawyer Jorge Reyes, stated that this announcement shows that the health authorities of the government are acting in opposition to the current legal situation, where the public distribution of EC pills is banned.

Scientific Evidence

At the same time, scientists and reproductive health advocates have expressed strong support for expanded access to EC in Chile. "Those opposed to this emergency contraceptive are a group of people that call themselves 'pro-life,' who are well organized and have significant power and influence," said Dr. Soledad Diaz, president of the Chilean Institute of Reproductive Medicine (ICMER). "They have a very stubborn doctrinaire position that doesn't want to recognize the scientific evidence that says the pill is not abortive. It's an ideological position, there is no other explanation."

Research and medical opinion back them up. The World Health Organization states, for example that "levonorgestrel emergency contraceptive pills (ECPs) have been shown to prevent ovulation and [do not] have any detectable effect on the endometrium (uterine lining) or progesterone levels when given after ovulation. ECPs are not effective once the process of implantation has begun, and will not cause abortion."

New Zealand Provides Free Long-Term Contraception for Welfare Recipients

Claire Trevett

Claire Trevett is a staff writer for the New Zealand Herald. *In the following viewpoint, she reports that a key part of the New Zealand government's welfare reform proposals is the availability of free long-term contraception for women on welfare, including teenagers and daughters of beneficiaries. This proposal is meant to ensure that women on welfare would not have any children while on benefits, instead focusing on improving their education or training to find a dependable and well-paying job. Trevett points out that opponents of the reforms argue that the measure is state interference into women's reproductive choices and express concern that women will be coerced into taking contraception.*

As you read, consider the following questions:

1. According to Trevett, how much was the budget package for the government's welfare reform?
2. How much of the package does Trevett report will pay for long-term contraceptive methods?

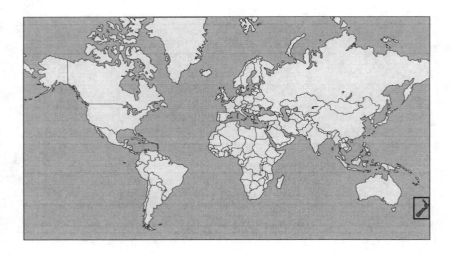

3. What is the total cost of reforms over a four-year period
   that will impose more stringent work-testing requirements on most welfare beneficiaries?

Women on benefits—including teenagers and the daughters of beneficiaries—will be offered free long-term
contraception as part of a $287.5 million budget package for
the government's welfare reforms.

But critics say the measure borders on state control of
women's reproductive choices.

Social Development Minister Paula Bennett and Prime
Minister John Key announced the package yesterday [May 7,
2012], aimed at supporting beneficiaries to get into training
or work.

It includes $1 million to pay for long-term contraception
measures such as implants or intrauterine devices [IUDs].

The payment for contraception will be offered to teenagers
on benefits from July [2012]. From October, it will be offered
to all women on benefits, and their daughters aged 16 to 19.

Yesterday, Ms Bennett said the funding for the reforms
would be heavily targeted at youth and teen parents, who were

most at risk of staying on benefits long term and having more children while on welfare.

The reforms include a requirement for those who have another child while on a benefit to look for work when that baby is 1, rather than wait until he or she is 5.

Ms Bennett said given that the government was introducing penalties for those who had further children while on a benefit, it needed to ensure there was better access to contraception.

"We certainly have concerns about children being born to those on welfare and we see the access to contraception as being a barrier, particularly the cost around it."

She said it would be voluntary.

[Social Development Minister Paula] Bennett said the funding for the reforms would be heavily targeted at youth and teen parents, who were most at risk of staying on benefits long term and having more children while on welfare.

State Control of Women's Bodies—Critics

However, Sue Bradford of the Auckland Action Against Poverty group said the measure bordered on state control of women's reproductive choices. The former Green MP [member of Parliament] said although it was billed as voluntary, there was a power imbalance between beneficiaries and case managers, who were under new pressure to get people back into work.

"My fear is that they will be pressured and intimidated into going along to the appointment for contraception. There are many in the church and community groups who believe that the state should not play a role in women's reproductive lives."

A Good Place to Raise Children

In 2012, New Zealand ranked among the five best places in the world to be a mother in the State of the World's Mothers report from Save the Children, an independent organization dedicated to promoting the health and welfare of mothers and children around the world. The annual mothers index report compares conditions for mothers in 165 countries based on factors such as health, education, nutrition, and the economic status of women. New Zealand placed fourth on the list in 2012 (after Norway, Iceland, and Sweden).

"New Zealand," Global Issues in Context Online Collection, 2012.

Greens co-leader Metiria Turei agreed, telling Newstalk ZB [a New Zealand radio station] this morning [that] providing free contraception is not the role of the state.

She questioned whether the initiative would be as voluntary as the government has promised.

"Any experience with the welfare system will tell you that staff will be encouraged to encourage women to take up the injection or IUD or similar, and there will be pressure on these young women to do that."

Insulting Options

Rebecca Occleston, from the Beneficiary Advisory Service in Christchurch, told Radio New Zealand it was "insulting" the way beneficiaries were being targeted.

"I think they are putting it in a way that implies that people on benefits are having children deliberately, so here, have some contraception, that will stop the problem.

"I think that is a bit simplified."

Ms Occleston said people on lower incomes also struggled to afford some contraception options.

"I think contraception should be free, or affordable, for everybody who wants or needs it," she said.

"I think if it wasn't worded in such an offensive way then it would probably be quite a good programme."

Pharmac already funds several contraceptive devices, including one brand of implant and IUDs, but Ms Bennett said for some women there was a cost to put in the devices or they could not use the approved options for medical reasons.

"We'll pay for the doctor's visit and the cost of the contraceptive itself where the cost is not fully funded by Pharmac."

Targeting Teen Parents?

Ms Bennett said she made no apology for targeting teen parents.

"Under the old system, 16- to 18-year-old teen parents were handed a sum of money every week and left to get on with it. This will change."

Yesterday's $287.5 million is part of the expected $520 million cost of reforms over the next four years that will impose more stringent work-testing requirements on most beneficiaries. The cost is about half of the expected savings from the reforms, estimated at $1 billion.

It includes $80 million for early childhood education and child care assistance payments, $55.1 million for 155 Work and Income staff dedicated to support people back into work, and $148.8 million for youth services.

The prime minister said the government had been upfront about the costs of its reforms, but said it was vital to support beneficiaries into work.

Youth and solo parents are the target of the first tranche of reforms.

Russian Women Turn to Abortion Because of the Cost of Contraceptives

Chloe Arnold

Chloe Arnold is a correspondent for Radio Free Europe/Radio Liberty (RFE/RL). In the following viewpoint, she reports that abortion remains the most popular form of birth control in Russia despite a range of new family planning options. A lack of awareness and the prohibitive cost of such options have led most Russian women to rely on abortion as their only choice when it comes to birth control. Health officials are concerned about the long-term health and emotional effects of multiple abortions on Russian women, including such complications as infertility. Part of the problem, according to Arnold, is that sex education is not part of the national curriculum and cultural attitudes inhibit discussion of sexuality and family planning strategies. A campaign to educate health professionals about modern methods of birth control has led to lower abortion rates in some regions of Russia.

As you read, consider the following questions:

1. According to Arnold, how many abortions were performed in Russia in 2006?

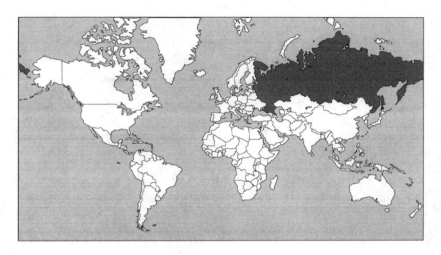

2. What percentage of Russian women does Arnold report use the birth control pill as their primary form of contraception?

3. According to Natalia Vartapetova, what percentage of infertility among Russian women is due to previous abortions?

Dilyara Latypova is a gynecologist in the Russian republic of Tatarstan. With more than 25 years of experience, she's seen some progress in family planning since the days of the Soviet Union, when such topics were largely taboo.

Still, she says, the situation today is far from ideal. For many women, the most common method of birth control remains a Soviet-era holdover: abortion.

Abortion as Birth Control

"Young women who think that having an abortion is an easy thing are wrong," Latypova tells [Radio Free Europe/Radio Liberty's] RFE/RL's Tatar-Bashkir Service. "An abortion is not only an operation. It's a deep psychological trauma for a woman. This is an operation that causes a woman physical and moral pain. I don't think it's the right decision."

Despite an abundance of new family planning options, Latypova says lack of public awareness and prohibitive expenses—like $25 monthly packs of birth control pills—mean many women still see abortion as their only choice.

"Students and young girls can't afford birth control. Many girls are afraid to talk about it with their mothers and ask for money," she says. "An unplanned pregnancy can cause them enormous stress. They immediately opt for an abortion, and don't even tell their parents or boyfriends."

Russia was the first country in the world to legalize abortion, in 1920. The procedure was briefly driven underground, when Soviet leader Joseph Stalin banned abortion in an attempt to encourage women to have larger families.

But after Stalin's death in 1953, the ban was lifted. A decade later, the practice had become so common that the USSR [Union of Soviet Socialist Republics, or Soviet Union] officially registered 5.5 million abortions, compared to just 2 million live births.

The relative ease of getting an abortion, in fact, has blinded many women to the numerous health risks associated with the process, especially for those who turn to it more than once.

A Private Matter

The number of abortions has fallen dramatically since then. The most recent available figures, for 2006, show 1.6 million abortions compared to 1.5 million live births—a dismal figure, especially in a country struggling with a looming demographic crisis.

Women are entitled to abortions up until the 12th week of pregnancy, and—unlike in many countries—are not obligated to alert relatives or give a reason for requesting the procedure.

The relative ease of getting an abortion, in fact, has blinded many women to the numerous health risks associated with the process, especially for those who turn to it more than once. "The complications include bleeding and inflammation in the short term," says Lyubov Yerofeyeva, the director of the Russian Family Planning Association, an NGO [nongovernmental organization] that works to improve sex education in Russia. "In the long term, the most severe complication could be infertility."

Part of the reason abortions were so prevalent during the Soviet era, health professionals say, was that contraceptives were so unreliable.

Yerofeyeva is speaking in a brightly lit office in central Moscow whose walls are adorned with posters of cuddly babies. But Yerofeyeva and other association employees can also paint a stark picture of the reality of abortion in Russia today.

Sex education is not part of the national curriculum in Russia. So when most young people become sexually active, at around the age of 16, Yerofeyeva says they know almost nothing about how women become pregnant.

"You can't say the idea of family planning and birth control is flourishing," she says. "The tradition in Russia is not to talk about sexuality loudly, not to tackle these issues—even within a family, even between husband and wife. Sometimes they're not even communicating about their own sexual relations. These issues have always been very closed."

Growing Options

Part of the reason abortions were so prevalent during the Soviet era, health professionals say, was that contraceptives were so unreliable. Oral contraception was not available and more often than not, Soviet-made condoms and intrauterine devices [IUDs] didn't work.

In the years after the Soviet collapse, before the expense grew too great, some gynecological clinics attempted to pro-

---

A Brief History of Russia

In medieval times, Russia was known as the principality of Muscovy and was ruled by a series of monarchs known as tsars. Tsarist rule continued in Russia until the revolution of 1917, which overthrew the tsar. A few years later, the Communist state was established and Russia became part of the Soviet Union, or USSR [Union of Soviet Socialist Republics]. The Soviet Union became a dominant world power during the twentieth century, especially during the Cold War period during which the United States and the USSR fought for influence and power throughout the world. The Soviet Union crumbled in 1991 and the Russian Federation was established. Though Russia initially emerged from communism willing to liberalize its system of government, the government has increasingly undermined democratic institutions and freedoms in addition to consolidating power in the executive branch.

"Russia," Global Issues in Context Online Collection, 2012.

---

vide birth control for free, a practice that has proved successful in places like the United Kingdom. The number of Russian women who use the pill as their primary form of birth control remains low—between 3 and 13 percent, as compared to 52 percent in Europe. The predominant form of preventive birth control is the highly uncertain rhythm method. But Vladimir Shchigolev at the Moscow office of the World Health Organization says the situation is improving.

"At the moment, the younger generation knows more about family planning, and they have better access to family planning services. Today, they can go to the pharmacy and buy contraceptive pills, condoms, modern IUDs that are quite different from Soviet IUDs—they are absolutely safe," Shchigolev says. "Of course they talk about abortion, but they talk about abortion as not a good way to prevent pregnancy and to plan a family."

Abortion techniques have come a long way since the Soviet era, when 35-year-old Olga Lipovskaya related her experience in Francine du Plessix Gray's acclaimed book *Soviet Women: Walking the Tightrope.*

"You stand in line before the door of the operating room, waiting to be taken in," she says. "Then it's your turn, and you go into a hall splattered with blood, where two doctors are aborting seven or eight women at the same time; they're usually very rough and rude. If you're lucky they give you a little sedative."

According to du Plessix Gray, Olga estimated that she had had about 14 abortions in total, and she knew women who had had as many as 25.

"Huge Psychological Trauma"

Today, modern techniques make the experience less traumatic and dangerous, but Natalia Vartapetova, the director of a Russian NGO called the Institute [for] Family Health, says complications following abortions are still widespread.

"Unfortunately, still, the consequences of abortion are among the key causes of maternal mortality in Russia," she says. "One of the problems, perhaps, is infection control— infection and sepsis afterward—or other complications, like hemorrhage. Infertility, as well—we know about one-third of infertility is due to previous abortions."

But for all that, the situation is improving, Vartapetova says. One of her projects is to educate health professionals about modern methods of birth control, and in the 20 or so regions where the programs are taking place, abortion rates have fallen.

Population Decline

And with the population level in severe decline—demographers estimate it could fall below 100 million by 2050, from 150 million in 1992—the Russian government is also keen to tackle the issue of abortion. Last year [in 2007], then president Vladimir Putin introduced a long-term project to encourage women to have families with more than one child.

The pro-Kremlin youth group Nashi this year staged a demonstration to protest abortion, adorning rows of cemetery-style crosses with signs reading "architect," "driver," "editor," and other professions—a nod to the potential labor lost to terminated pregnancies. (Nashi's conservative social streak extends to birth control; the group has protested against condoms and other preventive family planning methods.)

Vartapetova warns that attempts to prevent abortions or to restrict access to birth control would be a mistake. "When we talk about the demographic crisis, quite often there's a misunderstanding—that family planning leads to smaller family size. International evidence shows that that's not true—and that family planning actually improves women's health and decreases abortion rates. But this information isn't that well known among our policy makers."

Doctors like Latypova in Tatarstan are also quick to remind women of the enormous emotional cost that abortion can inflict. While the topic of abortion does not spark the kind of fierce moral debate seen in countries like the United States, Latypova says terminating a pregnancy can be a devastating experience.

"You can't compare the emotional state of a woman who undergoes an abortion with anything else. As both a doctor and a mother, I can say that it's a huge psychological trauma. There are very few women who can just breezily say, 'oh, I had an abortion.' I think there's no abortion that doesn't leave its mark on a woman."

Senegal: "Small Revolution" in Family Planning

Integrated Regional Information Networks (IRIN)

Integrated Regional Information Networks (IRIN) is a news agency that focuses on humanitarian subjects in developing and troubled regions. In the following viewpoint, IRIN suggests that there is a growing acceptance of family planning in Senegal, once known for its high fertility rate. One of the central reasons that contraception is widely accepted is the high cost of living in the country. Another reason is the success of government programs in national hospitals and clinics that encourage family planning. IRIN explains that Senegalese government officials hope to accomplish two goals: decrease maternal mortality and lower the fertility rate. To accomplish these goals, IRIN concludes, officials have made access to birth control a priority.

As you read, consider the following questions:

1. According to the health ministry, what was the birthrate in Senegal in 2009?
2. According to Marie Stopes International (MSI), what is the fertility rate in Dakar?
3. According to MSI, what will be the financial benefits from the recent opening of three family planning clinics in Senegal?

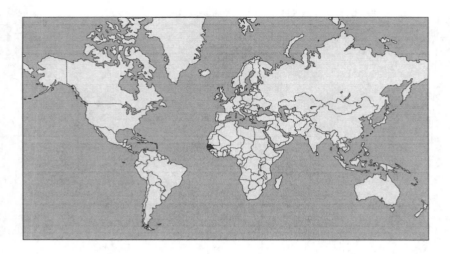

Talibouya Ka, Muslim leader (imam) of the Omar Kan mosque in the Medina neighbourhood of the Senegalese capital Dakar, encourages his followers to procreate as much as they can. "There are imams who are for family planning, but I am not. I tell worshippers they need to increase the size of the global Muslim family."

Such attitudes, which used to be prevalent in Senegal, are increasingly rare, particularly in Dakar, midwives and doctors at the Hospital Centre for Health and Hygiene in Medina, told IRIN.

Senegalese families are spacing their children, having fewer, and as a result are increasingly searching for long-term family planning solutions, said Fatou Seck, a midwife at the hospital.

While in 1990 the average woman in Senegal had 6.7 children in her reproductive cycle; in 2009 when the latest statistics were made available, they had 4.8, according to the health ministry.

"There is a small revolution going on—husbands and imams who were traditionally against any kind of family planning are slowly starting to accept it," said Ephie Diouf, 31, a child-minder in Dakar and mother of a five-month-old son.

Government Push

One reason for contraceptive take-up is the high cost of living, particularly in the capital, said Soda Diagne, 32, a Dakar businesswoman who is married without children. "People are realizing they can't feed and educate five children at today's prices." The price of imported rice—a staple in Senegal—rose sharply in 2007 and 2008 and then again in 2010.

While the average fertility rate across the country is five children per woman, in Dakar it is 3.9, according to NGO Marie Stopes International (MSI).

But the behaviour shift is also due to a push by the government to encourage family planning in state-run hospitals and clinics as part of its maternal mortality reduction strategy, said the UN Population Fund's (UNFPA) Senegal joint director Edwige Adekambi.

Many of the poorest performers in maternal mortality are in West Africa; while Senegal is at the high end of the regional scale, the numbers are still significant: 410 women die per 100,000 live births, according to the UN Children's Fund (UNICEF).

The health ministry has doubled the budget for reproductive health, and within that, has doubled the budget for family planning to US$200,000 per year, according to UNFPA.

At parliamentary level, politicians are also starting to take into account the need to balance economic and demographic growth, she added. (In many West African states, the potential gains of economic growth are being erased by soaring populations.)

Stock Ruptures

Part of the additional funding will be used to ensure that contraceptives start to be included in the list of essential stocks routinely ordered for government pharmacies and medical centres, as per a ministerial order.

To date, erratic supplies have severely impeded the ability of some women to access contraceptives, said Adekambi, which also means they are subject to paying more than the government-set tariff—100 CFA (20 US cents) for one month's supply of the birth control pill.

Diouf backs this up. She pays 1,500 CFA ($3.10) to a private pharmacy for her monthly contraceptive pill because her local clinic is often out of stock. "Many women I know go to private clinics to get their birth control pill, but end up taking bad or old pills and get pregnant anyway," she said. Availability is even lower in rural areas, where just one in 20 sexually active people use contraception (versus one in five in Dakar).

Since 2006 Catholic and Muslim religious leaders have worked together to try and issue updated religious guidelines on family planning, stressing the fact that neither the Koran nor the Bible are against spacing of births.

On 19 September, MSI opened three family planning clinics: two in the capital and one in M'Bour, 70km south of Dakar, aiming to give women greater access to affordable family planning services, as well as to give advice and testing on sexual health, and provide basic antenatal care. Providing these services at an affordable fee could reduce medical expenses linked to reproductive health in Senegal by $20.8 million by 2015, estimates MSI.

The government has been very supportive of the NGO's work, said Senegal director Maaika Van Min; and the local imam attended the opening ceremony of one of the new clinics.

Agents for Change

But while attitudes are changing, there are still pockets where people cling to traditional beliefs, said Adekambi, particularly in rural areas such as Matam in the northeast, which has the lowest contraceptive use rate in the country.

Since 2006 Catholic and Muslim religious leaders have worked together to try and issue updated religious guidelines on family planning, stressing the fact that neither the Koran nor the Bible are against spacing of births.

Midwife Seck said the imam at her local mosque now preaches to families to space their children by 30 months. "He tells families this is how to keep their wives healthy. Family planning is not banned in Islam. . . . Religion is about well-being, and spacing children is part of that."

In Matam, UNFPA worked with couples from the community to become agents for change: They went door to door to discuss family planning with household members. Contraceptive use has risen in the region, but Adekambi said nonetheless, UNFPA may take the approach one step further—by opening a "school for husbands" based on a model they organized in Niger, where reproductive sexual health and other gender issues are discussed.

Many husbands or partners are reluctant to embrace family planning at first, said midwife Seck. At consultations "we discuss with them the benefits . . . that their wife will have more time to look after each child, more time to look after herself, and most importantly, more time to look after him," she told IRIN.

That tactic often seems to do the trick, she said.

Periodical and Internet Sources Bibliography

The following articles have been selected to supplement the diverse views presented in this chapter.

Ben Agande   "FG Considers Legislation on Birth Control,"
                      Vanguard, June 27, 2012.

Eleanor Beardsley   "In France, Free Birth Control for Girls at Age
                      15," NPR, December 18, 2012. http://www.npr
                      .org/2012/12/18/167253336/in-france-free-birth
                      -control-for-girls-at-age-15.

Chinwuba Iyizoba   "Africa Needs Population Growth, Not Birth
                      Control," *Crisis*, May 25, 2011.

Steven W. Mosher   "Make Health Care, Not Birth Control, the
                      Priority," *Pacific Standard*, August 12, 2012.

Katie Rogers   "Contraception, Healthcare and the Costs
and Ruth Spencer   Women Will Leave Behind," *Guardian*, August
                      17, 2012.

Samira Shackle   "China's One-Child Policy Puts a Price on
                      Human Life," *New Statesman*, July 12, 2012.

This Day   "Preparing for Population Boom," December
                      11, 2012.

Yeganeh Torbati   "Iran Aims for Baby Boom, but Are Iranians in
                      the Mood?," Reuters, November 14, 2012.
                      http://www.reuters.com/article/2012/11/14
                      /us-iran-population-idUSBRE8AD0UZ20121114.

Henry Wasswa   "'Enough Is Enough': The Ugandan Men
                      Opting to Have Fewer Children," *Guardian*,
                      November 26, 2012.

Kenneth R. Weiss   "China's Population and Economy Are a
                      Double Whammy for the World," *Los Angeles
                      Times*, July 22, 2012.

For Further Discussion

Chapter 1

1. How does the availability and affordability of birth control affect population growth? Read the viewpoints in the chapter to inform your answer.

2. Tania Branigan outlines the problems with China's strict one-child policy in her viewpoint. In your opinion, should governments be setting and enforcing birth control policies? Why or why not?

Chapter 2

1. After reading the viewpoints in this chapter, what are some political reasons that governments would want to limit access to birth control? Explain in detail.

Chapter 3

1. Should religious authorities have influence on birth control policy? Why or why not?

2. The viewpoints in this chapter explore the ways in which religious authorities both encourage and discourage contraceptive use. What influence do religious authorities have in your community when it comes to family planning and birth control? Do you agree or disagree with this influence? Explain.

Chapter 4

1. How has the global economic downturn impacted family planning and birth control? Read the viewpoints in the chapter to inform your answer.

Organizations to Contact

The editors have compiled the following list of organizations concerned with the issues debated in this book. The descriptions are derived from materials provided by the organizations. All have publications or information available for interested readers. The list was compiled on the date of publication of the present volume; the information provided here may change. Be aware that many organizations take several weeks or longer to respond to inquiries, so allow as much time as possible.

Advocates for Youth

2000 M Street NW, Suite 750, Washington, DC   20036
(202) 419-3420 • fax: (202) 419-1448
website: www.advocatesforyouth.org

Advocates for Youth is an organization that works in the United States and developing countries to create responsible and effective sexual health strategies for adolescents and to disseminate accurate information about contraception, sexually transmitted diseases (STDs), and reproductive health. The ultimate goal is to provide young people with the tools they need to make responsible decisions about sexual behavior and family planning. One of the organization's key initiatives is the Adolescent Contraceptive Access Initiative, which focuses on offering accurate information on birth control options for young people. The Advocates for Youth website has a range of publications available, including reports, fact sheets, training materials for volunteers, and assessments of various programs around the world. There is also a blog, which features news and updates on current events sponsored by the organization as well as podcasts from experts and staff that discuss programs and policy debates.

Center for Reproductive Rights

120 Wall Street, New York, NY   10005

(917) 637-3600 • fax: (917) 637-3666
e-mail: info@reprorights.org
website: reproductiverights.org

The Center for Reproductive Rights is a global legal center that works to secure women's reproductive rights and access to contraception and family planning services. To this end, it has presented and defended cases before national courts, United Nations committees, and regional human rights bodies. The center also works with policy makers and legislators to strengthen reproductive laws in the United States and around the world. The group's website features access to a range of in-depth reports, press releases, surveys, fact sheets, policy briefs, and information on reproductive law and policy. Also available is *ReproWrites*, the center's monthly e-newsletter, which provides updates on recent initiatives and current news.

International Consortium for Emergency Contraception (ICEC)

588 Broadway, Suite 503, New York, NY   10012
(212) 941-5300
e-mail: info@cecinfo.org
website: www.cecinfo.org

The International Consortium for Emergency Contraception (ICEC) is an association of seven international family planning organizations working to ensure that women have access to safe and effective emergency contraception. ICEC's advocacy efforts are focused in four main areas: emergency contraception and youth; legal challenges; improving and ensuring access; and providing services to women in crisis situations. The ICEC publishes a biannual newsletter that features updates on its advocacy and legal efforts, announces upcoming events, and covers relevant issues.

International Planned Parenthood Federation (IPPF)

4 Newhams Row, London   SE1 3UZ
   England
+44 (0)20 7939 8200 • fax: +44 (0)20 7939 8300

e-mail: info@ippf.org
website: www.ippf.org

The International Planned Parenthood Federation (IPPF) is a global family planning organization. Its mission is to "improve the quality of life of individuals by providing and campaigning for sexual and reproductive health and rights (SRHR) through advocacy and services, especially for poor and vulnerable people." The IPPF works to ensure that women are not persecuted for pursuing family planning options and that women have access to a range of services that they can choose from when it comes to reproductive health. The availability and affordability of birth control is key to that mission. The IPPF website features blogs, press releases, and information on ongoing programs and initiatives all over the world.

Ipas
PO Box 9990, Chapel Hill, NC   27515
(919) 967-7052 • fax: (919) 929-0258
e-mail: info@ipas.org
website: www.ipas.org

Ipas is an international nongovernmental organization (NGO) that advocates for safe and accessible abortion services for women who need and want them and to end preventable deaths and injuries from unsafe abortion practices. A key part of the organization's mission is ensuring that women receive counseling and contraception to prevent further unwanted pregnancies. Ipas trains doctors, nurses, and counselors to provide comprehensive abortion care and researches the impact of improved contraceptive and abortion services in many areas. The Ipas website offers access to this research as well as blogs, commentary, and recent news in the field.

Marie Stopes International
1 Conway Street, Fitzroy Square, London, England   W1T 6LP
+44 (0)20 7636 6200 • fax: +44 (0)20 7034 2369
e-mail: info@mariestopes.org
website: www.mariestopes.org

Marie Stopes International is a global nongovernmental organization (NGO) dedicated to providing a full range of quality sexual and reproductive health services to poor and vulnerable women around the world. The organization often collaborates with governments, health care providers, academic institutions, and other NGOs and aid groups to provide comprehensive training, advocate for improved reproductive and contraceptive policies, and strengthen existing systems. Its website offers access to the organization's e-newsletter as well as research, statistics, and information on relevant programs.

National Family Planning & Reproductive Health Association (NFPRHA)

1627 K Street NW, 12th Floor, Washington, DC   20006
(202) 293-3114
e-mail: info@nfprha.org
website: www.nfprha.org

The National Family Planning & Reproductive Health Association (NFPRHA) is a membership organization that advocates for health care administrators and professionals who serve low-income patients in the family planning and reproductive health field. It also works to provide training and continuing education for its members. NFPRHA is committed to providing high-quality, federally funded family planning care. The organization's website offers access to press releases, videos, and family planning profiles, which chronicle the work NFPRHA does to help patients across the United States.

Planned Parenthood Federation of America

1110 Vermont Avenue NW, Suite 300, Washington, DC   20005
(202) 973-4800 • fax: (202) 296-3242
website: www.plannedparenthood.org

Planned Parenthood Federation of America is a nonprofit organization that provides reproductive health and family planning services. Planned Parenthood can be traced back to 1916, when family planning pioneer Margaret Sanger opened the country's first birth control clinic in Brooklyn, New York. Today, Planned Parenthood operates more than eight hundred health centers across the country that focus on high-quality and affordable health care. Another mission of Planned Parenthood is to educate American youth accurately and honestly about birth control choices and provide access to legal contraception. The organization publishes a number of fact sheets, studies, and news reports that can be found on its website.

United Nations Population Fund (UNFPA)

605 Third Avenue, New York, NY   10158
(212) 297-5000 • fax: (212) 370-0201
e-mail: hq@unfpa.org
website: www.unfpa.org

The United Nations Population Fund (UNFPA) is the United Nations agency tasked with improving the lives of women all over the world by advocating for gender equality and universal access to family planning services, including birth control and abortion care. The ultimate goals of UNFPA are to reduce the number of unwanted pregnancies, improve sexual and reproductive health, and decrease rates of maternal mortality. UNFPA "also focuses on improving the lives of youths and women by advocating for human rights and gender equality and by promoting the understanding of population dynamics. Population dynamics, including growth rates, age structure, fertility and mortality and migration have an effect on every aspect of human, social, and economic progress." The UNFPA website features access to recent news, a range of research and other publications, and information on the organization's services and programs.

US Department of Health and Human Services (HHS)

200 Independence Avenue SW, Washington, DC   20201
(877) 696-6775
website: www.hhs.gov

The Department of Health and Human Services (HHS) is the US government agency in charge of protecting the health of and providing essential health services to all Americans. HHS works closely with state and local governments to develop programs and implement policies. It is the goal of HHS to have a variety of safe and effective birth control options for American women and provide accurate and up-to-date information on such products. The HHS website offers a series of fact sheets on different birth control options as well as other educational information.

US Food and Drug Administration (FDA)

10903 New Hampshire Avenue, Silver Spring, MD   20993
(888) 463-6332
website: www.fda.gov

The Food and Drug Administration (FDA) is an agency of the US Department of Health and Human Services (HHS) tasked with protecting public health through the testing, regulation, and supervision of contraception, prescription and over-the-counter medications, food safety, biopharmaceuticals, medical devices, and more. The FDA is in charge of testing and regulating the new emergency contraception that has come on the market. The agency also determines how birth control will be available. Information on how such decisions are made as well as press releases and studies can be found on the FDA website.

World Health Organization (WHO)

Avenue Appia 20, 1211, Geneva 27, Switzerland
(+41) 22 791 21 11 • fax: (+41) 22 791 31 11
e-mail: info@who.int
website: www.who.int

The World Health Organization (WHO) is the United Nations agency responsible for directing global health care matters. WHO funds research into health issues that affect global health, including contraception and reproductive health. The agency monitors health trends, compiles useful statistics, and offers technical support related to reproductive health services to countries worldwide. The WHO website features podcasts, blogs, and videos; it also offers fact sheets, reports, studies, and a calendar of events. There are a broad range of articles on contraception on its website, including reproductive health, services, and availability.

Bibliography of Books

Jean H. Baker — *Margaret Sanger: A Life of Passion.* New York: Hill and Wang, 2011.

Barbara Bonnekessen — *Of Homunculus Born: A Short History of Invisible Women.* Lanham, MD: University Press of America, 2012.

Allan Carlson — *Godly Seed: American Evangelicals Confront Birth Control, 1873–1973.* New Brunswick, NJ: Transaction Publishers, 2012.

Laura Eldridge — *In Our Control: The Complete Guide to Contraceptive Choices for Women.* New York: Seven Stories Press, 2010.

Jessica Fields — *Risky Lessons: Sex Education and Social Inequality.* New Brunswick, NJ: Rutgers University Press, 2008.

Angel M. Foster and Lisa L. Wynn, eds. — *Emergency Contraception: The Story of a Global Reproductive Health Technology.* New York: Palgrave Macmillan, 2012.

Susan K. Freeman — *Sex Goes to School: Girls and Sex Education Before the 1960s.* Urbana: University of Illinois Press, 2008.

Christine J. Gardner — *Making Chastity Sexy: The Rhetoric of Evangelical Abstinence Campaigns.* Berkeley: University of California Press, 2011.

Miriam Grossman — *You're Teaching My Child What?: A Physician Exposes the Lies of Sex Education and How They Harm Your Child.* Washington, DC: Regnery, 2009.

Melissa Haussman — *Reproductive Rights and the State: Getting the Birth Control, RU-486, Morning-After Pills and the Gardasil Vaccine to the U.S. Market.* Santa Barbara, CA: Praeger, 2013.

Rose Holz — *The Birth Control Clinic in a Marketplace World.* Rochester, NY: University of Rochester Press, 2012.

Nicholas D. Kristof and Sheryl WuDunn — *Half the Sky: Turning Oppression into Opportunity for Women Worldwide.* New York: Alfred A. Knopf, 2009.

Alexandra M. Lord — *Condom Nation: The U.S. Government's Sex Education Campaign from World War I to the Internet.* Baltimore, MD: Johns Hopkins University Press, 2010.

Kekla Magoon — *Sex Education in Schools.* Edina, MN: ABDO, 2010.

Elaine Tyler May — *America and the Pill: A History of Promise, Peril, and Liberation.* New York: Basic Books, 2010.

Leonard J. Nelson III — *Diagnosis Critical: The Urgent Threats Confronting Catholic Health Care.* Huntington, IN: Our Sunday Visitor, 2009.

Carl Olson, ed.   *Celibacy and Religious Traditions.* New York: Oxford University Press, 2008.

Shawn Lawrence Otto   *Fool Me Twice: Fighting the Assault on Science in America.* New York: Rodale, 2011.

Heather Munro Prescott   *The Morning After: A History of Emergency Contraception in the United States.* New Brunswick, NJ: Rutgers University Press, 2011.

Isabella E. Rossi, ed.   *Abstinence Education.* New York: Nova Science Publishers, 2009.

Rickie Solinger   *Reproductive Politics: What Everyone Needs to Know.* New York: Oxford University Press, 2013.

Guang-zhen Wang   *Reproductive Health and Gender Equality: Method, Measurement, and Implications.* Burlington, VT: Ashgate, 2010.

Index

Geographic headings and page numbers in **boldface** refer to viewpoints about that country or region.

Y

Z